CITYSPOTS

WARS

WHAT'S IN YOUR GUIDEBOOK?

Independent authors Impartial up-to-date information from our travel experts who meticulously source local knowledge.

Experience Thomas Cook's 165 years in the travel industry and guidebook publishing enriches every word with expertise you can trust.

Travel know-how Contributions by thousands of staff around the globe, each one living and breathing travel.

Editors Travel-publishing professionals, pulling everything together to craft a perfect blend of words, pictures, maps and design.

You, the traveller We deliver a practical, no-nonsense approach to information, geared to how you really use it.

CITYSPOTS

WARSAW

Alex Webber

Thomas Cook

Written by Alex Webber with contributions from Sco and Andrew Quested
Original photography by Don Eggington
Front cover photography (Warsaw Mermaid) © Siegfried Layla/Getty Images
Series design based on an original concept by Studio 183 Limited

Produced by Cambridge Publishing Management Limited
Project Editor: Ross Hilton
Layout: Paul Queripel
Maps: PC Graphics
Transport map: © Communicarta Limited

Published by Thomas Cook Publishing
A division of Thomas Cook Tour Operations Limited
Company Registration No. 1450464 England
PO Box 227, Coningsby Road
Peterborough PE3 8SB, United Kingdom
email: books@thomascook.com
www.thomascookpublishing.com
+ 44 (0) 1733 416477

ISBN: 978-184157-747-0

Series/Project Editor: Kelly Anne Pipes
Production/DTP: Steven Collins

Printed and bound in Spain by GraphyCems

CONTENTS

SYMBOLS KEY

The following symbols are used throughout this book:

@ address ⓣ telephone ⓦ website address
◷ opening times ⓝ public transport connections ❗ important

The following symbols are used on the maps:

i information office	O city
✈ airport	O large town
+ hospital	○ small town
police station	motorway
railway station	main road
M metro	minor road
✝ cathedral	railway

❶ numbers denote featured cafés & restaurants

Hotels and restaurants are graded by approximate price as follows:

£ budget ££ mid-range £££ expensive

▶ *The reconstructed buildings in the Old Town Square*

INTRODUCING Warsaw

Introduction

Warsaw, a city of nearly 2 million and capital of a resurgent Polish nation, is once again punching its weight as a major European city. Straddling the River Vistula, its location between the old powers of Germany and Russia has ensured that it has been a victim of history on more than one occasion. After the horrors of World War II, the Communist period saw the meticulous reconstruction of the city's historic buildings and a rash of Socialist Realist building. During the same time, cultural activity was suppressed and the spirit of the city forced underground.

Warsaw emerged from the Communist era determined to rejoin the European mainstream and shed its Eastern Bloc image. The transition to capitalism was painful at first, but Warsaw residents took to market economics with typical gusto. Poland joined the EU in 2004 and Warsaw is now in the midst of the greatest economic boom in its history.

Riding on the coat-tails of this new-found wealth is a renewed vigour in the city's cultural life. While it may not be able to rival Kraków's museums, galleries and historic legacy, Warsaw is the hub of modern Polish culture and it's where the trends and fashions are set. It is also Poland's centre of academia and the large student and young professional contingent has ensured one of Europe's most happening nightlife scenes.

Yet it's not all hip in Warsaw, and the grey tower blocks and cabbage soup are there if you want to find them – the city is a work in progress, with an energy and soul that is often compared to the Berlin of the 1990s. This 'gritty but groovy' edge is exactly what draws those in the know to the city. But don't take their word for it, check it out for yourself.

The onion domes of St Mary Magdalene

When to go

CLIMATE & SEASONS

Most visitors to Warsaw arrive in the summer months of June, July and August. You can expect afternoon temperatures of about 20–23°C (68–73°F), and usually a week or two of very hot weather in August with extremes of 30–35°C (86–95°F). Nights cool down, so have a sweater or light jacket handy. These three months are also by far the wettest of the year, with July peaking at 96 mm (3.8 in). Summer also means full hotels and crowded sights, but on the other hand the city is noticeably quieter as many locals head out into the countryside to enjoy the heat while it lasts.

May and June have pleasant daytime temperatures averaging 20–23°C (68–73°F) and a reduced chance of rain. Visiting in autumn is the second-best option. Warsaw's parks riot with colours and are stunningly beautiful in late September to early November. Temperatures are still good at 19°C (66°F) on average in September and 13°C (55°F) in October.

January and February are the bleakest months of the year, with short, grey days that remain between –6°C (21°F) and 0°C (32°F), though occasionally it can drop to –10°C (14°F) or –15°C (5°F). Snowfall changes the normally noisy city into a fluffy quiet dream with dampened sounds, and walking around town right after a fresh layer has fallen can be magical. Unfortunately, traffic soon grinds the snow to sludge and then pedestrian life becomes harder.

ANNUAL EVENTS

Warsaw may not have a packed calendar of festivals like its rival Kraków, but nevertheless has a number of interesting annual events, with most of them taking place in the summer months.

Spring

Ludwig van Beethoven Easter Festival Local and international musicians gather each Easter to honour the master in a series of concerts and related events. ⓦ www.beethoven.org.pl

Easter (8 April 2007 & 23 March 2008) Poland's most important religious festival is celebrated with church services and processions.

Wilanów Park in late summer

Anniversary of the Warsaw Ghetto Uprising 19 April – Flowers are laid at the Monument to the Ghetto Heroes to remember those who died in the 1943 uprising.

Summer

Chopin Memorial Sunday Concerts Every Sunday at 12.00 and 16.00, May to September – Polish pianists play homage to Chopin in Royal Lazienki Park. ⓦ www.chopin.pl

Mozart Festival (June & July) The Warsaw Chamber Opera performs Mozart, including all his stage works.
ⓦ www.operakameralna.pl

Noc Swiętojańska Midsummer's Eve marks the longest day of the year, with fireworks, food and girls throwing wreaths into the river.

International Street Art Festival (July) Streets, squares and parks become the stage for theatrical performances.

Jazz in the Old Town Saturdays in July & August
ⓦ www.muzyka.wp.pl/jazznastarowce

Musical Gardens (July & August) Films featuring opera, ballet and other musical arts are shown in the courtyard of the Royal Castle. ⓦ www.ogrodymuz.pl

International Chopin Festival (July & August) Poland's most famous composer is honoured with concerts.
ⓦ www.tifc.chopin.pl

Warsaw Summer Jazz Days (June to August) Free contemporary jazz concerts around town. ⓦ www.adamiakjazz.pl

Anniversary of the 1944 Warsaw Uprising (1 August) Commemorating the failed uprising of the Polish Home Army against the Nazis in 1944.

Autumn

Warsaw Autumn The Polish festival of contemporary music. www.warsaw-autumn.art.pl

Warsaw International Film Festival (Early October) More than 100 films from dozens of countries are shown. www.wff.pl

Winter

Warsaw Piano Festival (November) Piano concerts held over five days at the Royal Castle. www.beethoven.org.pl

PUBLIC HOLIDAYS

Banks and shops close on the following national public holidays, and don't be surprised to find many bars and restaurants following suit.

Note that the day sandwiched between 1 and 3 May, known as Majówka, is an unofficial public holiday.

New Year's Day 1 January
Easter Sunday and Monday March/April
State holiday (renamed from Labour Day) 1 May
Constitution Day 3 May
Corpus Christi May/June
Assumption of Virgin Mary and Polish Army Day 15 August
All Saints' Day 1 November
National Independence Day 11 November
Christmas Day 25 December
Boxing Day 26 December

Warsaw jazz

Although it comes as a surprise to most Western Europeans, jazz has a long tradition in Poland. Pre-war dance club bands in Warsaw and other cities got Poles moving to swing-based jazz in the 1930s. After World War II the Communist government suppressed the music and it was forced underground. During this so-called 'Catacomb Period', performances were confined to private homes and musicians risked arrest.

The death of Stalin in 1953 and the subsequent political thaw afforded jazz musicians a new-found freedom to perform in public. Five years later Dave Brubeck's visit to the country was to prove highly influential on the direction of the burgeoning jazz scene. In the early 1960s the first Warsaw Jazz Jamboree Festival was staged. Now called the JVC Jazz Festival Warsaw, it is one of the longest-running jazz festivals in Europe and has hosted many of the great names in jazz including Miles Davis, Thelonious Monk, Dizzy Gillespie and Ray Charles. It takes place every October in the awe-inspiring Palace of Culture and Science. See Ⓦ www.festivalproductions.net for further details.

Not content with just one jazz festival, Warsaw also plays host to the Warsaw Summer Days Jazz and the Jazz in the Old Town festivals. The latter is a series of free open-air performances in the Rynek (Main Square) of the Old Town and is held every Saturday evening in July and August. These concerts often attract large crowds and they are a great way to spend a balmy summer's evening in historic surroundings. See Ⓦ www.muzyka.wp.pl/jazznastarowce for more information.

If you happen to be in town when there isn't a jazz festival in full flow, there is a vibrant year-round jazz scene based around cafés, jazz clubs and concert halls to keep you occupied. Notable venues include **Jazz Bistro** (ⓐ ul. Piwna 40 ⓣ 022 887 87 64 ⓦ www.jazzbistro.pl,) **Jazz Café Helicon** (ⓐ ul. Freta 45/47 ⓣ 022 635 95 05) and **Blender Bar** (ⓐ pl. Piłsudskiego 3 ⓣ 022 331 89 00 ⓦ www.blenderbar.pl)

Warsaw's JVC Jazz Festival is held at the Palace of Culture & Science

History

Warsaw's early history is vague – there's evidence of a 10th-century village here, though the current city was probably founded in 1294, and became capital of Mazovia in 1413. Poland united with Lithuania in 1569, and the capital of the new Commonwealth was moved from Kraków to Warsaw by King Sigismund II Augustus, with the royal court following in 1611. From 1700–21 the Great Northern War with Sweden and Russia weakened the Commonwealth so much that it was effectively run by Russia. In the following decades, Poland disappeared from the map completely. The first partition of the country, in 1773, saw Prussia, Russia and Habsburg Austria helping themselves to 30 per cent of the Commonwealth's territory. The three powers took more territory in 1793 and 1795, eventually carving up Poland entirely between themselves, ending its independence for 123 years.

Napoleon briefly came to the rescue when he created the semi-independent Duchy of Warsaw en route to Moscow in 1807, though his defeat meant Russia took control again in 1813. Only at the end of World War I did Poland free itself from occupation on 11 November 1918.

History turned against Poland once more in 1939 when Germany and the Soviet Union agreed to split the country again. On 1 September, World War II began with the shelling of a small garrison near Gdańsk. In 1943, the Jews in Warsaw's Ghetto staged an uprising that was brutally ended with the complete destruction of the district after almost a month of fighting. A year later, the Polish underground Home Army started the Warsaw Uprising, hoping for support from the Soviets and conquering much of the city. After two months of bitter fighting, the Poles surrendered. Hitler ordered the evacuation and complete destruction of the city, and buildings were dynamited in order of their cultural importance.

The Red Army finally liberated Warsaw in January 1945: 85 per cent of the city was in ruins, 80 per cent of the historical buildings had been completely destroyed, and 700,000 people were dead. Rebuilding started immediately after the war, and, in 1980, the city's painstakingly reconstructed Old Town was added to UNESCO's World Heritage List.

Under the Communist People's Republic of Poland there was nationalisation of companies and private and Church property, while intellectuals and religious leaders were imprisoned. The Polish Cardinal Karol Wojtyła was elected Pope in 1978 and visited his home country soon after. Poland's bankrupt economy started showing cracks in the 1970s, and shipyard worker Lech Wałęsa co-founded the Solidarność (Solidarity) trade union. The government cracked down by declaring martial law in 1981, but it was too late and, from 1985, liberalisation (helped by Gorbachev's *perestroika*) took place. In 1989 the Communist regime collapsed. Post-Communist Poland joined NATO in 1999 and became an EU member state in 2004.

Lifestyle

Warsaw is the wealthiest city in Poland, though the disparities in income can, at times, be painfully obvious. Life is easy for the privileged few, but for others the trials of the capitalist world mean juggling several jobs, or, in many cases, migrating westwards to other EU countries where the financial rewards are higher. Wages in Poland remain much lower than in the west, though Warsaw easily rates as one of the more expensive cities in the central/eastern European region. Many people will continue to live with their parents well into their 20s, but, no matter what their social standing may be, the younger locals are a well-dressed bunch and in summer the streets can resemble a catwalk, as the local fashionista trot in between bars and restaurants. Western material culture has made a deep

COMMON COURTESY

When it comes to common etiquette, the locals can be a funny bunch. Queues have no apparent logic and it's every man for himself, yet failing to surrender your seat on the tram to the elderly is seen as an almost criminal act. Always hold the door open for someone else and never refuse the offer of a vodka – unless it comes from a shady-looking character. Finally, do remember the Poles are a deeply religious people. The institution of the Catholic Church is held in high esteem and should not be mocked or disparaged in any way, no matter what your religious inclinations are.

impact on the city and the young seem happy to sacrifice the freedom of living on their own in favour of having the latest camera phone, handbag, Japanese gadget or exotic holiday.

Those arriving expecting to live in the lap of luxury in return for a bag of buttons face disappointment. A night spent in the better restaurants and bars is not necessarily that much cheaper than what one may already be used to. However, this does little to stop the natives enjoying themselves and the city offers the bubbling social atmosphere shared by all the great capitals. The only time this is not outwardly obvious is when the city simmers in the August heat and many of the locals choose to flee town for less stifling climes.

Café culture is alive and well in the city

Culture

Warsaw is where everything exciting happens, where the money is, where all the 'jet-set' live and work, and where the big exhibitions unfold. Whereas culture in Kraków , with its 'cultural capital of Poland' tag, is mainly focused on foreign tourists and on Poles going to see royal relics, Warsaw's cultural scene is young, vibrant, daring and isn't afraid to poke fun at authority and tradition. With 2 million inhabitants, Warsaw has plenty to offer for culture vultures, be they local or foreign.

Foreigners will not be able to grasp much of the Polish-language theatre productions in town, but there is ample opportunity to enjoy other genres, such as opera and classical music. Before its destruction in World War II, Warsaw was a royal, baroque city and it has seen many composers and performers come and go. Chopin is Poland's most famous composer, and his music can be heard at the festival and the famous piano competition dedicated to him as well as at concerts held throughout the year. Don't forget that the churches scattered around the Old Town and beyond also often put on concerts, be they organ recitals, choral singing or orchestral works. Jazz enthusiasts won't be disappointed in Warsaw – there is a healthy appetite for both traditional and progressive jazz and all its other forms in Poland, with many artists and bands performing year-round in smoky cafés, jazz clubs and concert halls. Several jazz festivals are held each year in Warsaw.

Due to its near-destruction in the war, Warsaw's cultural heritage is not as visible as in well-preserved cities, and when touring the city it can be hard to get a feeling of scale, history

Street sculpture courtesy of an old town gallery

and local culture. Therefore, a good city tour – preferably with a private guide – can really help you to understand the city and its inhabitants, more so than by wandering around the Old Town by yourself. Once you see the city in the light of its historical turmoil, you'll appreciate the museums, statues and memorials dedicated to its main events, heroes and heroines. Even if you're not a war buff, a visit to some of the memorials and museums can really be an eye-opener into the logic behind the local culture of stubborn resistance.

Note that the season for performances ends in June and begins again in September or October – just after the summer when tourists are most likely to visit. Fortunately, there are ample special events and festivals to enjoy over the summer months, and of course all museums remain open as usual during this time.

Warsaw's tourist information office can provide more details about what's on when, or see the events section in the *Warsaw In Your Pocket* city guide Ⓦ www.inyourpocket.com or the *Warsaw Insider* Ⓦ www.warsawinsider.pl

The modern face of Polish consumerism – Galeria Mokotow shopping mall

MAKING THE MOST OF Warsaw

Shopping

Warsaw offers a wide range of shopping opportunities to everyone from bargain-hunters to spendthrifts. The majority of designer stores can be found clustered around pl. Trzech Krzyży with most brands around 20 per cent cheaper than their British counterparts. Close by, the area stretching from ul. Mokotowska to Krakowskie Przedmieśćie is where you'll find the finest antique stores, though check out the old town as well. Shopping malls are prevalent, with the best being **Galeria Mokotów** (ⓐ ul. Wołoska 12 ⓦ www.galeriamokotow.pl) and **Arkadia** (ⓐ al. Jana Pawła II 82 ⓦ www.arkadia.com.pl)

The most famous market is the **Russian Market** (◷ 06.00–14.00 Mon–Sun), found on the Praga side of

SHOPPING FOR SOUVENIRS

A bottle of vodka is always a safe bet, with brands like Chopin and Belvedere proving the most popular. For something a little different, check out the shop Nalewki I Inne inside the Arkadia mall, which sells a variety of herbal and fruit vodkas. Poland is also famous for its amber, and many of the stores in and around the old town sell this fossilised resin. Polish glassware has also made a name for itself, and once again your best source for this will be the old town and the area around Nowy Świat. Bear in mind that if a product was made before 1945 you may need a special document, available from the retailer, allowing you to take it out of the country.

Poniatowskiego bridge, in and around the environs of Stadion Dziesięciolecia. Reputedly Europe's largest outdoor market, this is Warsaw's primary source for counterfeit and bootlegged goods and makes for a fascinating excursion. Of course, watch your wallet at all times. For something more highbrow check out **Baza Na Kołe** (ⓐ ul. Obozowa 99 ◷ 06.00–14.00 Sat & Sun). This is where you'll find antique curiosities ranging from World

Folk crafts for sale on a market stall

War II memorabilia to 19th-century globes. Bargaining is essential to get the best deal. Photographers should make a beeline for the **Photo Market** at (ⓐ ul. Batorego 10 ⓑ 10.00–14.00 Sun). Here you'll find banks of stalls inside the Stodoła nightclub selling discounted camera equipment ranging from the latest top-range bits and pieces to ancient Soviet LOMOs.

USEFUL SHOPPING PHRASES

What time do the shops open/close?
O której godzinie otwierają/zamykają, sklepy?
O ktoo-rey go-jee-nyair otvyerayom/za-me-ka-yom skhle-pe?

How much is this?
Ile to kosztuje?
Ee-lair toh ko-shtoo-yeh?

Can I try this on?
Czy mogę to przymierzyć?
Che mo-ghair toh pshe-mye-jech?

My size is ...
Mój rozmiar to . . .
Mooy roz-myarh toh . . .

I'll take this one, thank you
Poposzę o to
Po-pro-shair o toh

This is too large/too small/too expensive. Do you have any others?
To jest zbyt duże/zbyt male/zbyt drogie. Czy macie coś in-ne-go?
Toh yest zbit doo-jeh-zbit ma-weh/zbit dro-ghyeh. Che ma-che cosh in-ne-go?

Eating & drinking

Polish food is a simple, filling affair. Starters include a range of tasty soups such as *żurek* (a sour rye soup) and *barszcz* (beetroot) and more traditional restaurants will serve up a plate of bread and *smalec* (lard) as a complimentary prelude to your meal. One particular Polish speciality to look for is *piergoi*, a ravioli-style offering filled with either meat or cabbage and sometimes even with seasonal fruit. Polish sausages, otherwise known as *kiełbasa*, are famous the world over, and for good reason, while the local game dishes also impress. For the hardcore immersion experience, order a bowl of *bigos*, a thick, foul-smelling stew comprising meat, cabbage and sauerkraut.

To enjoy Polish food the real way then visit one of the milk bars (*bar mleczny*) that stubbornly refuse to die. You'll need to place an order with the monolingual lady before claiming your winnings through a hatchway. Quite often what you'll receive will resemble little more than a steaming plate of mashed objects, though you'll pay next to nothing for the honour. Aside from these interesting relics of the past, Polish restaurants tend to fall into two categories: rustic themed ventures with staff dressed as peasants and hunks of pigs served on wooden boards, or upmarket efforts with well-presented nouvelle takes on Polish dishes.

PRICE RATING

Throughout the guide we have used the following pricing code for a three-course meal for one without drinks.

£ under 50 zł **££** 50–100 zł **£££** over 100 zł

Warsaw's international popularity has led to an explosion of new cuisines arriving in the capital, with sushi and fusion food being the most popular. Practically every venue will have an English menu, and English-speaking service is guaranteed in all but the old-school restaurants. Most restaurants open their doors at 12.00 and will continue cooking until the last customer leaves.

A traditional Polish restaurant

TIPPING

The art of tipping can present problems for the first-time visitor. Unfortunately in Poland many waiting staff take thanking them as they collect your cash as a sign that you are delighted with the service you have received – and that they can therefore keep all the change. This habit is slowly dying out as more and more waiters return with experience gained from working in the West, though it's still advisable to remain tight-lipped when handing money over – unless of course you have no wish to see your change. Check any small print on your bill that indicates a service charge; if none is apparent then it is normal to reward good service either by rounding up your bill or by leaving 10 per cent. It's down to you. Bear in mind that while service has improved dramatically over the years, and it is now rare to be met by rude staff slamming plates in front of you, many have yet to catch on to the concept that the customer is king, and

VODKA CUSTOMS

Leaving Poland without sampling the joys of vodka is a sin. Don't dare suggest that the Russians invented it, and instead busy yourself with local mainstays like Wyborowa, Chopin and Belvedere. Vodka should be drunk chilled, neat and in one go, so don't even think of asking for a dash of orange juice unless you want to face ridicule. If you must dilute your vodka with a soft drink then opt for a Żubrówka – vodka flavoured with bison grass and mixed with apple juice. Do as the Poles do and keep your stomach lined by snacking on herring in between shots.

seem to have no qualms in disappearing to write text messages or have a laugh with their mates behind the scenes. If faced with slack service, bear no guilt for failing to leave a tip.

USEFUL DINING PHRASES

I would like a table for ... people
Poprozę o stolik dla ... osób
Po-pro-shair o sto-leek dla ... o-soob

May I have the bill, please?
Poproszę o rachunek?
Po-pro-shair o ra-hoo-neck?

Waiter/waitress!
Kelner/Kelnerka!
Kelner/Kelnerka!

Could I have it well cooked/medium/rare, please?
Poproszę o dobrze/średnio/lekko wysmażone?
Po-pro-shair o do-bjeh/shre-dnyo/lek-ko ve-sma-jo-ne?

I am a vegetarian. Does this contain meat?
Jetsem wegetarianinem/wegetarianką (fem.). Czy w tym daniu jest mięso?
Yestem vegetarianinem/vegetariankahng (fem.). Tchee fteem dah-nyoo yest myensoh?

Where is the toilet (restroom), please?
Przepraszam, gdzie jest toaleta?
Pshe-pra-sham ghjair yest toe-a-lair-tah?

Entertainment & nightlife

As befits a capital city, Warsaw offers a rich and varied social life with something to please every taste, from the conservative to the eccentric. There is no particular centre for nightlife, rather numerous areas with clusters of nightspots. On the whole the area from pl. Trzech Krzyży running up to pl. Teatralny is where most nightclubbers will find themselves. In particular, ul. Foksal, Nowy Świat, Sienkiewicza and the area around pl. Teatralny have had a heap of bars and clubs sprout up, and you'll find the garden furniture coming out at the first hint of summer. One worrying development is the number of velvet ropes found outside venues; many clubs and bars will operate a 'door-selection policy' that, at times, can prove fiercely bitchy. If you're looking to drink in the better establishments then ensure you make an effort on your appearance, as otherwise you may find yourself facing snidey insults from the fashion police guarding the entrance – and, believe us, playing the foreigner-with-lots-of-money card will not work. Although Warsaw is not the 24-hour city that, say, London or Paris is, venues do tend to stay open late with bar staff usually working until the last customer decides to leave. Friday is the biggest night out, so don't be surprised to find Saturday nights quiet in comparison; this is when many locals choose to get out of the city for the weekend, especially in summer. On a drinking note, do not under-estimate the potency of Polish beer. Most lagers average at around the 5.5 per cent mark and, when paired with a few of the local vodkas, disaster can strike. If you're not up to a hair of the dog then visit a pharmacy (*apteka*) to pick up a hangover cure.

Entertainment comes in many guises

If your pleasures are a little more cerebral then you'll find plenty to occupy you. Pretty much all the shopping malls come equipped with a multiplex cinema, though the most comfortable option is the **Silver Screen** at (ⓐ ul. Puławska 17 ⓦ www.silverscreen.pl). For something more esoteric try the **Muranów cinema**, an independent cinema with a reputation for showing cult classics (ⓐ ul. Gen. Andersa 1 ⓦ www.muranow.gutekfilm.com.pl). Films are usually shown in their original language with Polish subtitles, the only exception being kids' films, which are dubbed. For a full list of cinemas and what's showing check ⓦ www.warsawinsider.pl

Astonishingly, Warsaw is yet to boast an international-sized and standard concert venue and many of the biggest bands choose to play their concerts at the national arena in Chorzów (southwest Poland). Warsaw does attract big names, but they'll usually play at the Palace of Culture and Science, the racetrack or the Legia football stadium. You can book online at ⓦ www.ticketonline.pl and ⓦ www.eventim.pl, though neither have English versions of their websites. The big branches of EMPiK Megastore also sell tickets for most of the key events going on in Warsaw. Find their flagship store at ⓐ ul. Nowy Świat 15–17 ⓦ www.empik.com

Come summer, visitors have a wealth of open-air events to choose from, including an annual gay parade (no firm dates), jazz festivals in the old town square and orchestral recitals beside the Chopin statue in Łazienki Park. Those wishing to witness a piece of Polish theatre should bear in mind that theatres close every summer.

The University of Warsaw Botanical Gardens are a great place to unwind

Sport & relaxation

Aside from strong-man competitions and ski-jumping, sporting greatness has largely eluded Poland in recent years. Like most of the civilised world, the number one spectator sport in the country is football, though fans of the national side have had little to crow about. Nonetheless passions still run high. The local team, Legia Warszawa, are the biggest side in Poland and, though their crowds rarely exceed 10,000, a visit to one of their games promises a cracking atmosphere. Although their immediate derby rivals are Polonia Warszawa, the true hatred is reserved for Wisła Kraków, a team that has dominated the domestic game in recent years. For fixture lists and ticket info visit ⓦ www.legia.com. Sadly, hooliganism is still commonplace in Poland, as is racist chanting; it's advisable to sit in the expensive seats to avoid the more rough and ready elements of the crowd.

Most of the top-flight hotels feature spas, fitness centres and swimming facilities, with the pick of the bunch being the 5-star InterContinental Hotel with its 40th-floor swimming pool. If you don't have the resources to stay in one of the top-flight hotels then visit **Wodny Park** (ⓦ www.wodnypark.com.pl), a great complex with a multi-lane Olympic swimming pool, as well as separate areas with water slides and wave machines. Several entertainment complexes with bowling, pool tables and other such diversions have sprouted up across town, with one of the most popular being the centrally located **Hula Kula Leisure Centre** (ⓐ ul. Dobra 56/66 ⓣ 022 552 74 00). Shoot around in go-karts at **Imola** (ⓐ ul. Puławska 33 ⓦ www.imola.pl) or go quad-biking at the **Adrenalin Factory** (ⓐ ul. Modlińska 342 ⓦ www.fabrykaadrenaliny.pl). All-year ice-skating can be found at the **Torwar Ice Rink** (ⓐ ul. Łazienkowska 6a ⓦ www.towar.pl) and a free outdoor rink springs up each winter outside the **Palace of Culture and Science** (ⓐ pl. Defilad 1).

A game of roller hockey in the city centre

Accommodation

Ever since cracks started appearing in the Iron Curtain, Warsaw has assumed the role of one of the major financial markets in the central European region. As a result there's no shortage of top-class hotels, and you'll find numerous new boutique hotels as well as 5-star skyscrapers reaching for the skies, each trying to outsize the other.

For those travelling without a laptop and expense account, accommodation at the lower end of the scale is scandalously limited, and advance bookings are essential. Occupying the middle ground are chain efforts such as Ibis and Novotel, while the local mid-table brand, Orbis hotels, have undertaken serious surgery to pull themselves into line; the prostitutes have been cleared out of the lobbies, and Brezhnev-era aesthetics switched in favour of a sharp western look. With only two hostels worth genuine consideration, it's backpackers who have the most to fear: most hostels in Warsaw transpire to be off-season student digs with scabby quarters and awkward locations, so it's recommended to book a place at either the Oki Doki or Nathan's Villa well in advance.

Now, the good news. Come the weekend, Warsaw's hotels empty, meaning most enter a price war in a bid to draw the tourist traffic. Check the websites of individual hotels for special

PRICE RATING

All prices are for a single night in a double or twin room.

£ up to 200 zł **££** 200–500 zł **£££** over 500 zł

offers, or alternatively shop around on websites like Ⓦ www.staypoland.com or Ⓦ www.hotelspoland.com for the most competitive rates. You'll be surprised how affordable even the premier efforts become; it's not unknown to pay as little as 50 euros per night in return for a 5-star pampering. On a final note, do your geography before making any bookings. While most hotels are located in the centre, the spread-out nature of Warsaw means it's effortlessly easy to end up idling away your time listening to the wisdom of a taxi driver – ensure your hotel is near to where you want to spend your time.

HOSTELS

Nathan's Villa Hostel £ Poland's leading hostel, some say, and the praise and awards that Nathan's has scooped add credence to the claim. Opened in 2004, this hostel leaves ticks in all the boxes of a backpacker's wishlist: high-speed internet access, sparkling living quarters, fully stocked kitchen and a laundry service that doesn't lose your socks. Brand new private rooms have been added for those wishing to escape the hedonistic air of dormitory life. ⓐ ul. Piękna 24/26 ⓣ 022 622 29 46 Ⓦ www.nathansvilla.com

Oki Doki £ The gloomy entrance does no justice to a hostel that bursts with individuality. Rooms are the work of the local Boho set, and tout names like 'The House of Kitsch Deer in Rutting Season'. You can sleep in a room filled with pictures of commie parades, or opt for one with Beatles LPs pinned to the walls. Both private and dorm facilities are on offer, with amenities including internet, kitchen and soundproofed walls that

Unusual sculpture in the lobby of Hotel Novotel Centrum

guarantee you won't be disturbed by party animals.
ⓐ pl. Dąbrowskiego 3 ⓣ 022 826 51 12 ⓦ www.okidoki.pl

HOTELS

Premiere Classe £ Clean beds and not much more inside this 1-star bargain. Low-cost box rooms are kept meticulously clean, otherwise the perks are limited to ensuite showers and television. Hugely popular with local businessmen whose salaries have yet to be renegotiated, so book well in advance if you want a bed during the week. ⓐ ul. Towarowa 2 ⓣ 022 624 08 00 ⓦ www.premiereclasse.com.pl

Grand Hotel Orbis ££ A superb socialist structure that has seen a new lease of life under the Orbis hotel group. Impressively illuminated in the evenings, this hotel offers staple 3-star standards that prove unfailingly popular with package tours and group bookings. ⓐ ul. Krucza 28 ⓣ 022 583 21 00 ⓦ www.orbisonline.pl

Ibis ££ The hotel equivalent of fast food. You won't find any surprises at the Ibis, and this one will be identical to any other you have stayed in. No points for originality, but full marks for consistency, good service and spotless, if bland, rooms. ⓐ ul. Muranowska 2 ⓣ 022 310 10 00 ⓦ www.orbisonline.pl

Old Town Apartments ££ An extremely flexible service with rooms ranging from well-kept modern units in the city centre, to huge studio flats inside the historic quarters of Warsaw's old town. A great choice for groups as well as solo travellers.

ⓐ Rynek Stareo Miasto 12/14 ⓣ 022 820 92 27
ⓦ www.warsawshotel.com

Le Regina £££ Indulge yourself at Warsaw's most exclusive hotel. Occupying a restored 18th-century property, this boutique hotel effortlessly combines all the creature comforts of the modern world with an air of luxurious serenity. ⓐ ul. Kościelna 12
ⓣ 022 531 60 00 ⓦ www.leregina.com

Rialto £££ A remarkable hotel with an art deco motif running from top to bottom. Glass mosaics, nickel-plated brass and furnishings plucked from the cream of Europe's antique houses fill individually designed rooms where themes range from jazz age New York to colonial Africa – complete with animal skins and tribal masks. Other amenities include a library, cigar room and one of the finest dining rooms in Warsaw. ⓐ ul. Wilcza 73
ⓣ 022 584 87 00 ⓦ www.hotelrialto.com.pl

THE BEST OF WARSAW

Whether you're lucky enough to have time to savour Warsaw over a few weeks or are just on a flying visit, there's more than enough to keep you interested. The following should be near the top of any itinerary.

TOP 10 ATTRACTIONS

- **Historical Museum of Warsaw** A magnificent foxtrot through Warsaw's highs and lows (see page 68).

- **The old town** A bewitching network of cobbled streets, church spires and hidden courtyards (see page 61).

- **Palace of Culture and Science** Stalin's gift to Poland, and one of the most notorious existing examples of Socialist Realist architecture (see page 80).

- **Pawiak Prison** A grim reminder of Nazi terror (see page 84).

- **Royal Castle** A symbol of Warsaw rebuilt (see page 66).
- **Russian Market** Europe's largest bazaar, and where mayhem and bargains collide (see page 99).
- **Traditional dining** Whether splashing out on an extravagant meal or a budget heap of sausages, don't leave Warsaw without trying the local delicacies (see page 27).
- **Warsaw's Jewish past** Retrace Warsaw's tragic past (see page 77).
- **Warsaw Uprising Museum** Warsaw's most heroic moment relived inside one of Poland's finest museums (see page 97).
- **Wilanów** A majestic palace likened to Versailles (see page 94).

▼ *Mural from the Communist period*

HALF-DAY: WARSAW IN A HURRY

Pushed for time? An afternoon is just about enough time to glimpse Warsaw's Jekyll and Hyde nature. Start off by visiting the Communist monstrosity otherwise known as the Palace of Culture and Science, and don't forgo a visit to the panoramic viewing platform at the top. Follow this by getting a cab up to the old town for a quick walk around its atmospheric streets, making enough time for a stop-off at Kompania Piwna for a gut-busting traditional meal.

1-DAY: TIME TO SEE A LITTLE MORE

As above, though more time on your hands means a proper opportunity to nose around the old town, with a visit to the Historical Museum of Warsaw, a must for those wishing to learn more about the city. Don't forget to stray north of the Barbakan to have a look around the new town area. Finish off with a visit to the Warsaw Uprising Museum, a powerful tribute to the heroism of those who died fighting for liberty. A visit here is not just for war buffs, but vital in understanding the very mechanics of modern Warsaw.

2–3 DAYS: SHORT CITY BREAK

Set aside a day to visit Wilanów, a supreme throwback to the days of Imperial Poland and packed with interesting exhibitions and collections. Do dress up and enjoy the clubs and bars of Warsaw, but be careful with the hangover in order to make an early morning visit to the Russian Market. Escape from the chaos and babble of a thousand tongues by walking through Warsaw's largest and most beautiful cemetery, Powązki, and don't miss the neighbouring Jewish Cemetery, a forlorn and thoughtful walk.

LONGER: ENJOYING WARSAW TO THE FULL

When you've done the above make time to potter around Warsaw's series of churches and cathedrals, many of which come dripping with stories and sacral art. Make the foray into the Praga district to see a side of Warsaw left off most itineraries, and while you're there, temper your sightseeing with a drawn-out coffee in one of the many artsy cafés that have sprung up inside this corner of Warsaw. With Warsaw now familiar territory, hop on a train out to Poland's second city, Łódź. Often nicknamed 'Poland's Manchester', this former textile town, a product of the Industrial Revolution, surprises all with its nightlife, culture and history. Travel that bit further to see Poznań, a picturesque town with a calming aesthetic, but thriving, social scene.

The Barbakan Tower and gate links the old town to the new

Something for nothing

You find yourself in a financially draining city and it's not hard to leave Warsaw with the similar feeling that overwhelms the majority when exiting a casino. But that's not to say it's impossible to enjoy Warsaw if you find yourself skint. First off, remember that most Polish museums are in the habit of waiving admission charges once a week, usually on a Sunday. Even better, many museums of martyrdom and national suffering are free all week round. To leave on good terms all you have to do is drop a few coins into the donations tin at the end. To view missiles, rockets and other boys' toys, visit the Polish Army Museum (ⓐ al. Jerozolimskie 3). You'll pay to view the disappointing displays inside, though it's free to walk around

ROYAL ROUTE

While Warsaw is not a city built for walking, it does have one noteworthy trail, notably the Royal Route, the road regents once travelled on their way to the Royal Castle in the old town. Start by casting envious glances at minted shoppers at the bottom of Nowy Świat, before continuing up Krakowskie Przedmieśćie and into the old town. No matter how may times you've seen them, the snaking streets of this quarter never fail to captivate, especially in summer when they fill with buskers singing for their supper. Failing that, cheat. Claim you've seen all of Warsaw by paying the 20 zł it costs to zoom up to the panoramic viewing tower on top of the Palace of Culture ⓐ pl. Defilad 1.

the exciting bits in the courtyard. If you need something a little more uplifting then explore the churches and cathedrals, of which Poland has no shortage, making sure not to miss St John's Cathedral. Save on time and costs getting around by investing in an all-day travel card (*bilet dobowy*), available from one of the kiosks for 7.20 zł. If you're here for longer then both three-day and one-week cards are also available.

Socialist Realist statues outside the Palace of Culture & Science

When it rains

Buy an umbrella. Warsaw lacks the underworld caverns and curiosities of towns like Kraków and Wrocław, and even if it didn't its sprawling size means you'd get soaked in the point that lies between A and B. The hard core will rough out weather extremes by repairing to one of the many world-class bars found around town, though others should consider journeying to one of Warsaw's galleries or museums. First on the list should be the **Zachęta National Gallery** (ⓐ pl. Małachowskiego 3 ⓦ www.zacheta.art.pl) whose imperious halls come stuffed with ever-changing displays of contemporary art, many of which feature some of the leading names in the art world. More avant-garde absurdities can be viewed in its sister gallery, the **Kordegarda**, (ⓐ ul. Krakowskie Przedmieśćie 15/17).

A visit to one of the principal museums should consume enough time to pass a downpour, though it's probably best advised to use inclement weather as a reason to visit lesser-known museums that would otherwise be bypassed. The Museum of Technology inside the **Palace of Culture & Science** (ⓐ pl. Defilad 1) is one such venue, and its labyrinth of draughty halls houses a dizzying assortment of gadgets including a German Enigma machine, a printing press dating from 1846 and a collection of Spectrums, Ataris and other distant relics from the computer age. For a similarly surreal experience take a trip to the **Firemen's Museum** (ⓐ ul. Chłodna 3), where aside from rows of fire engines and helmets visitors can wince at the startling sight of household objects recovered from local infernos. On a lighter note, head to the **Fryderyk Chopin**

Museum (ⓐ ul. Okólnik 1 ⓦ www.nifc.pl) to learn more about the life of Warsaw's pet composer. Set inside a baroque castle, exhibits to look at include the locally born Chopin's last piano, handwritten letters and period furniture.

The Zachęta National Gallery, first choice when it rains

On arrival

TIME DIFFERENCES

Poland is one hour ahead of Greenwich Mean Time. Clocks move forward one hour and back again on the last weekend in March and October respectively. Midday in summer in Poland means the time back home is as follows:

Australia Eastern Standard Time 20.00; Central Standard Time 19.30; Western Standard Time 18.00
New Zealand 22.00
South Africa 12.00
UK and Republic of Ireland 11.00
USA and Canada Newfoundland Time 07.30; Atlantic Canada Time 07.00; Eastern Time 06.00; Central Time 05.00; Mountain Time 04.00; Pacific Time 03.00; Alaska 02.00

ARRIVING

By air

Warsaw's Okęcie Airport (sometimes known as Fryderyka Chopina) lies to the southwest of the centre, about 20 minutes by taxi. In the arrivals hall ignore any sly-looking men purporting to be taxi drivers and head to the line of officially licensed taxis outside. If they've got big glowing logos and a list of fares pinned to the window, you can trust them. Your journey to the centre should cost between 25 and 40 zł, so enquire beforehand to avoid costly surprises.

Bus 175 runs frequently from around 05.00 until 23.00 – the bus stop lies just across from Terminal 1. Night bus 611 operates after 23.00, about twice an hour. Tickets (*bilety*) can be purchased from the kiosks inside the terminal and need to be validated by punching them into the yellow machines on boarding.

The majority of budget airlines fly to Warsaw Etiuda, a five-minute walk from the principal terminals. ATMs are available and once again be wary of unlicensed cab operators. Domestic flights leave from the building between Etiuda and Terminal 1.

By rail

Warsaw has three principal train stations: Zachodnia (West), Centralna (Central) and Wschodnia (East). International trains will tend to stop at all three. Centralna is the one you're most likely to need; the main ticket hall has numerous ATMs, exchange offices (*kantors*), a Tourist Information point, a 24-hour pharmacy and fast-food cabins. Polish Rail (PKP) also runs a superb multilingual office that can arrange train tickets, hotel rooms and taxis. Cabs can be found outside on the Marriott Hotel side of the station.

Travel in style around the old town

Warsaw
0 2 km
0 1 mile
ZOLIBORZ
Pl Wilsona
Citadel
Zoo
Gdańska
Dworzec Gdański
Arkadia
SŁONINSKIEGO
NEW TOWN
Warsaw Zoo
City Walls
Powązki Cemetery
Ratusz
Royal Castle
OLD TOWN
Koło
Świętokrzyska
Palace of Culture & Science
Powiśle
CITY CENTRE
WOLA
Kasprzaka
Centrum
Centralna
Glowna
Ochota
Wola
Zachodnia
OCHOTA
Politechnika
WAWELSKA
Pole Mokotowskie
MOKOTÓW
Racławicka
Wodny Park
Rakowiec
Wierzbno
SD Galeria
Wilanowska
Służewiec
Służew
Port Lotniczy im Fryderyka Chopina
RASZYN
Okęcie
ALEJA ARMII KRAJOWEJ
KS POPIE ŁUSZKI
WYBRZEŻE GDYŃSKIE
JAGIELLOŃSKA
MOST GDAŃSK
POWĄZKOWSKA
POWSLANCOW SLASKICH
PRYMASA TYSIACLECIA
OKOPOWA
JANA PAWŁA II
WYBRZEŻE GDAŃSKIE
AL SOLIDARNOŚCI
GÓRCZEWSKA
TOWA ROWA
WOLSKA
PROSTA
KASPRZAKA
AL JEROZOLIMSKIE
MARSZAŁKOWSKA
POLCZYNSKA WOLSKA
AL NIEPODLEGŁOŚCI
PUŁAWSKA
ALEJE JEROZOLIMSKIE
GRÓJECKA
ŻWIRKI I WIGURY
HYNKA
SASANKI MARYNARSKA
RZYMOWSKIEGO
ALEJA KRAKOWSKA
Metro Stop
Cathedral
Information
Airport
Railway Stn
Hospital

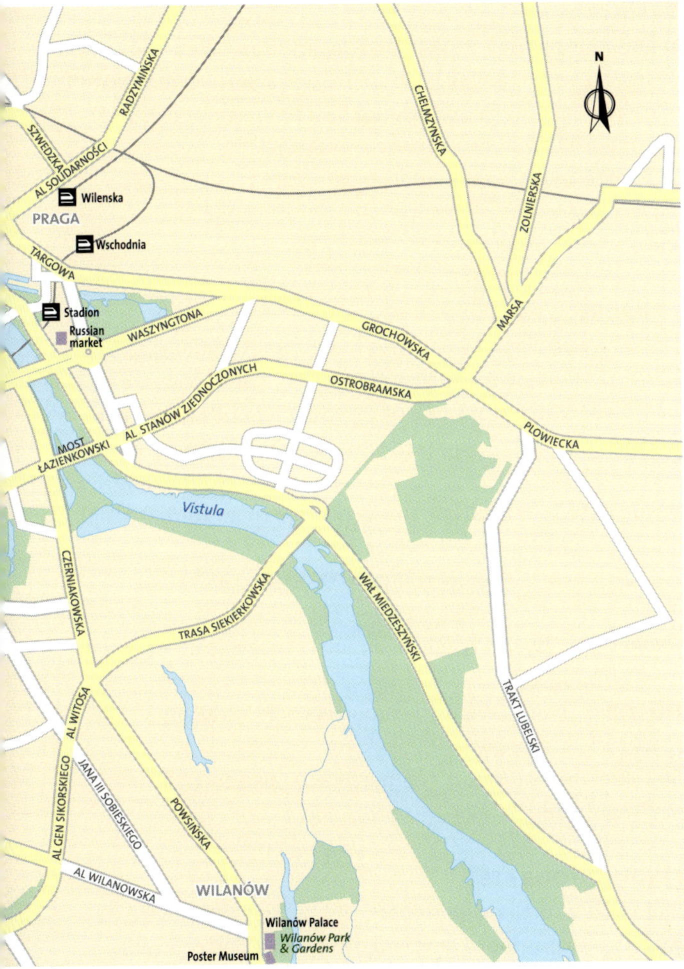
N
RADZYMIŃSKA
SZWEDZKA
AL SOLIDARNOŚCI
Wilenska
PRAGA
Wschodnia
TARGOWA
Stadion
Russian market
WASZYNGTONA
CHEŁMŻYŃSKA
ZOLNIERSKA
MARSA
GROCHOWSKA
OSTROBRAMSKA
AL STANÓW ZJEDNOCZONYCH
MOST ŁAZIENKOWSKI
PLOWIECKA
Vistula
CZERNIAKOWSKA
TRASA SIEKIERKOWSKA
WAŁ MIEDZESZYŃSKI
TRAKT LUBELSKI
AL WITOSA
AL GEN SIKORSKIEGO
JANA III SOBIESKIEGO
POWSIŃSKA
AL WILANOWSKA
WILANÓW
Wilanów Palace
Wilanów Park & Gardens
Poster Museum

By bus

International buses arrive at and depart from the car park by Warsaw Zachodnia train station (though some will terminate at the Palace of Culture and Science next to Warsaw Centralna). The main hall contains all the necessities: ATMs, currency exchange, tourist information, toilets and ticket kiosk. Taxis hover outside and will charge between 20 and 30 zł for a trip into the city centre.

CAR HIRE

Unless you're planning any trips to far-flung locations it's best to rely on cabs and/or public transport, as Polish roads are in bad shape. With an absence of speed cameras it's common to see cars zooming through red lights at breakneck pace. If you choose to take your chances then always carry your ID and documents. The speed limit inside Warsaw is 50 km/h (30 mph).

Avis ⓐ ul. Żwirki i Wigury 1 (airport) ⓣ 022 650 48 72
ⓦ www.avis.pl

Budget ⓐ ul. Żwirki i Wigury 1 (airport) ⓣ 022 650 40 62
ⓦ www.budget.pl

Hertz ⓐ ul. Żwirki i Wigury 1 (airport) ⓣ 022 650 28 96
ⓦ www.hertz.com.pl

Sixt ⓐ ul. Żwirki i Wigury 1 (airport) ⓣ 022 650 20 31
ⓦ www.sixt.pl

FINDING YOUR FEET

Warsaw is a seething metropolis and, on first appearance, its wide boulevards, loony drivers, dark subways and concrete towers can appear a little daunting. A good map followed by a firm idea of what you want from the city – whether it be bars or museums or both – are essential. The city is generally safe and well policed, though carrying expensive-looking gadgets and flapping maps around will draw attention to yourself, especially from the pickpockets who occasionally work the key bus and tram routes around the train station and airport.

ORIENTATION

This is a vast city and it's easy to lose yourself on unpronounceable streets and snaking subways. The most obvious landmark is the Palace of Culture & Science, which can be seen on a clear day from as far as 30 km (19 miles). Streets are clearly marked with

IF YOU GET LOST, TRY …

Excuse me, do you speak English?
Przepraszam, czy mówi Pan/Pani po angielsku?
Pshe-pra-sham che moo-vee Pan/Pa-nee poe an-gyels-koo?

Excuse me, is this the right way to the old town/ the city centre/the tourist office/the train station/ the bus station?
Przepraszam, czy dojdę tędy do starego miasta/ centrum miasta/biura turystycznego/dworzec kolejowy/ dworca autobusowego?
Pshe-pa-sham che doy-dair ten-di doe sta-re-go mya-stah/ sten-troom mya-stah/byoo-rah too-ri-sti-chne-go/ dvo-zhets ko-le-yo-vi/dvortsah awto-boo-so-vego?

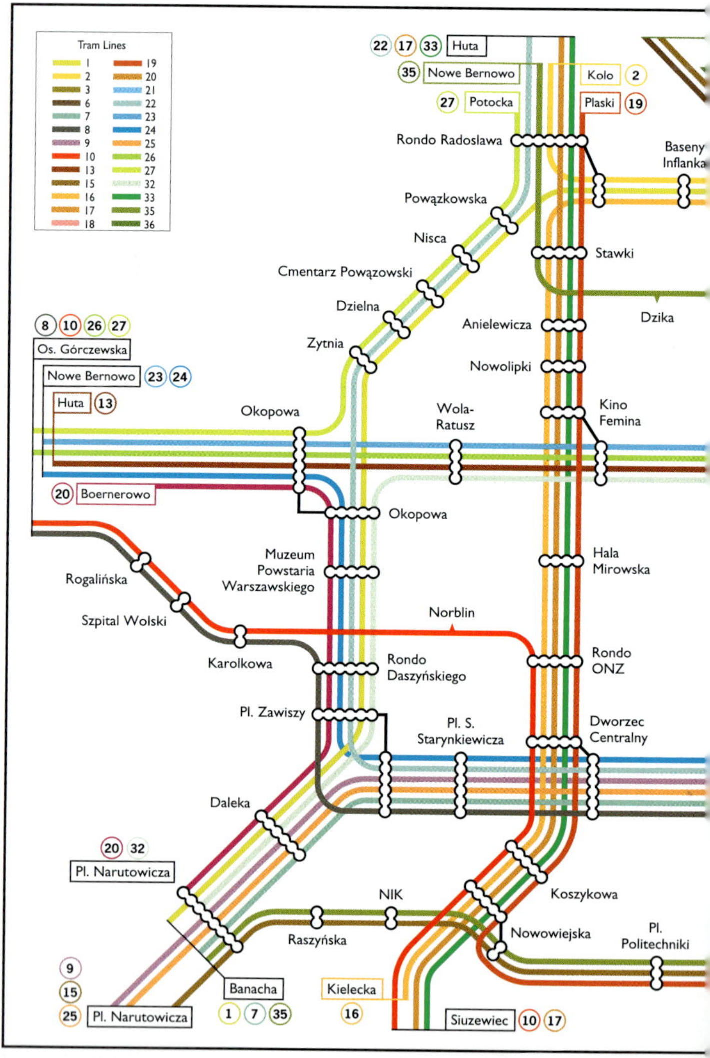
Tram Lines
1
2
3
6
7
8
9
10
13
15
16
17
18
19
20
21
22
23
24
25
26
27
32
33
35
36
22 17 33 Huta
35 Nowe Bernowo
27 Potocka
Kolo 2
Plaski 19
Rondo Radoslawa
Baseny Inflanka
Powązkowska
Nisca
Stawki
Cmentarz Powązowski
Dzielna
Dzika
Anielewicza
8 10 26 27
Os. Górczewska
Zytnia
Nowe Bernowo 23 24
Nowolipki
Huta 13
Okopowa
Wola-Ratusz
Kino Femina
20 Boernerowo
Okopowa
Muzeum Powstaria Warszawskiego
Hala Mirowska
Rogalińska
Szpital Wolski
Norblin
Karolkowa
Rondo Daszyńskiego
Rondo ONZ
Pl. Zawiszy
Pl. S. Starynkiewicza
Dworzec Centralny
Daleka
20 32
Pl. Narutowicza
NIK
Koszykowa
Raszyńska
Nowowiejska
Pl. Politechniki
9
15
25 Pl. Narutowicza
Banacha
1 7 35
Kielecka
16
Siuzewiec 10 17

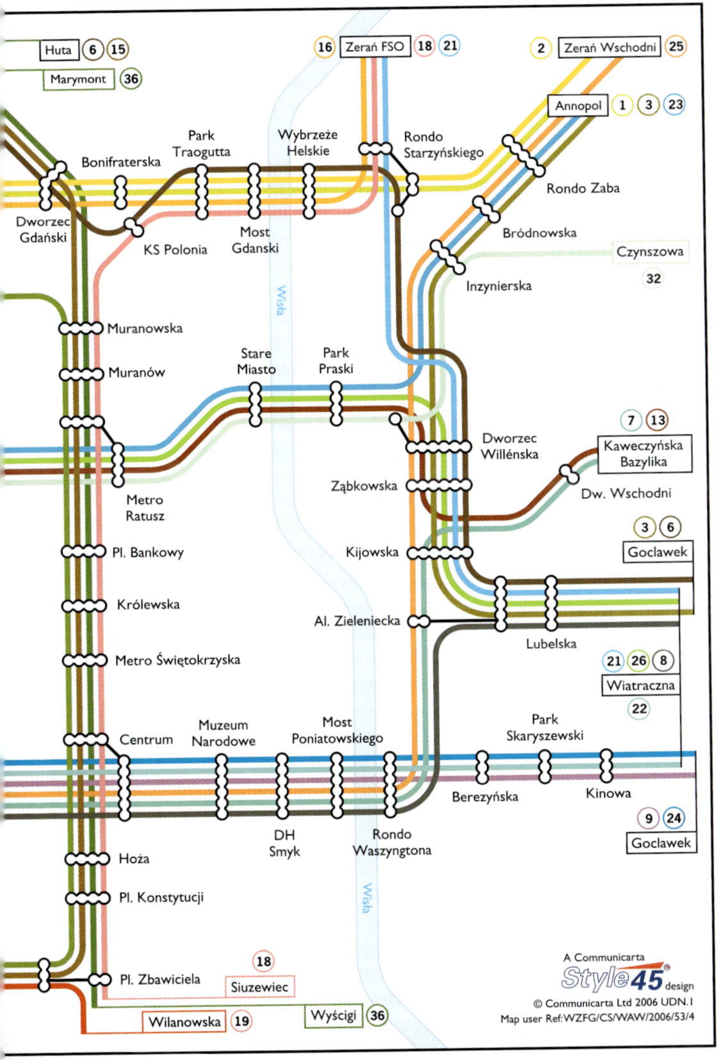
Huta 6 15
Marymont 36
16 Zerań FSO 18 21
2 Zerań Wschodni 25
Annopol 1 3 23
Park Traogutta
Wybrzeże Helskie
Rondo Starzyńskiego
Bonifraterska
Rondo Zaba
Dworzec Gdański
KS Polonia
Most Gdanski
Bródnowska
Czynszowa
32
Inzynierska
Wisła
Muranowska
Muranów
Stare Miasto
Park Praski
7 13
Kawęczyńska Bazylika
Dworzec Willénska
Ząbkowska
Dw. Wschodni
Metro Ratusz
3 6
Goclawek
Kijowska
Pl. Bankowy
Królewska
Al. Zieleniecka
Lubelska
Metro Świętokrzyska
21 26 8
Wiatraczna
22
Muzeum Narodowe
Most Poniatowskiego
Park Skaryszewski
Centrum
Berezyńska
Kinowa
9 24
Goclawek
DH Smyk
Rondo Waszyngtona
Hoża
Pl. Konstytucji
Wisła
18
Siuzewiec
Pl. Zbawiciela
Wilanowska 19
Wyścigi 36
A Communicarta Style45 design
© Communicarta Ltd 2006 UDN.I
Map user Ref:WZFG/CS/WAW/2006/53/4

red and blue signs, though this thoroughness does not always extend to house numbers. Cyclists can be a menace on pavements, and other hazards include icicles dropping on to your head during the thaw. To reach the old town from the city centre, it's best to start at the plastic palm tree that stands on the intersection of Nowy Świat and al. Jerozolimskie. Simply follow Nowy Świat northwards. Eventually the street becomes ul. Krakowskie Przedmieśćie, and you'll arrive at St Sigismund's Column. The old town lies right in front.

GETTING AROUND

Taxis are prevalent, though as mentioned before, only use clearly marked licensed cabs such as MPT (t 9191) or ELE (t 811 11 11). Warsaw is criss-crossed by a network of tram and bus routes and these represent the best and cheapest mode of transport. Buy tickets from any kiosk cabin or from the shops in your hotel. The tickets you buy are valid for all forms of public transport and must be punched into the yellow machines when you climb on board. Ticket inspectors appear at the most inopportune times and show no mercy towards foreigners. If you plan on using public transport frequently then one-day, three-day and one-week travel cards can also be purchased. Note that trams stop running at around 23.00, after which you'll be relying on night buses. If waiting for a night bus you will need to wave at the driver if you want him to stop. The Warsaw metro is superb, though with only one line running from north to south, it's of limited use to the tourist.

A lion guards the Royal Route

THE CITY OF Warsaw

The historic centre

If Warsaw's historic centre looks a bit too perfect, that's because it is. Suffering complete devastation in 1944, the reconstruction work was only completed in 1962 and now stands as a defiant symbol of a city that refused to die. While the rest of Warsaw resounds to the relentless sound of car horns, the fairytale backdrop of the new and old towns offers visitors an exquisite escape from the modern world.

SIGHTS & ATTRACTIONS

Citadel

Lying just north of the new town, Warsaw's Citadel was constructed in the wake of the 1830 November Uprising to serve as a fortress for the occupying Imperial Russian army. Housing a garrison of 16,000, the structure was also used as a political prison and a place of execution. Its twisting tunnels and cells have been carefully preserved, complete with the personal effects of former inmates – whose number include Rosa Luxemburg and Feliks Dzierżynski, who would later achieve notoriety as the founder of the Bolshevik secret police. The grounds contain modern military hardware, such as Soviet tanks and a Katyusha rocket launcher.
ⓐ ul. Skazańców 25 ⓣ 022 839 12 68 ⓛ 09.00–16.00 Wed–Sun, closed Mon & Tues

City walls

A set of defensive walls mark the boundaries of the old town, with the crowning glory being the Barbakan Tower – a gateway linking the new town with the old. Completed in 1548 using the designs of the Venetian architect Giovanni Battista, the 15-m-(49-ft-) high bastion was occupied by fusiliers and proved to be the scene of heavy fighting during the Swedish Deluge of 1656. As the centuries ticked by, the surrounding moat found itself being filled in and the walls and defensive tower gradually disappeared among the forest of new buildings constructed around it. During 1937 these impinging townhouses were pulled down so the Barbakan could once more be viewed in its full magnificence, though that would not last for long; Nazi bombardment during 1944 left the walls little more than scraps of rubble. Rebuilt in 1954, the Barbakan is now a paradise of street-sellers hawking their wares, while a walk around the walls reveals several monuments. Aside from the Little Insurgent (see page 64) the most striking of these is the sabre-wielding Jań Kiliński, a Polish cobbler who led local forces into battle against the Russians during the 1794 Kościuszko Uprising.

The old town

'Before and after' pictures from the wartime period tell all you need to know about the scale of destruction Warsaw suffered under Nazi rule. The rebuilding work carried out since has been painstaking and the old town's inclusion on UNESCO's World Heritage List is a fitting reward. Start any walking tour at the foot of St Sigismund's Column outside the Royal Castle. Erected in 1664 to honour the regent who shifted Poland's capital from Kraków to Warsaw, the 22-m (72-ft) structure collapsed during the war, though the original figure of Sigismund survived and now perches on the new column. If you want to see the old

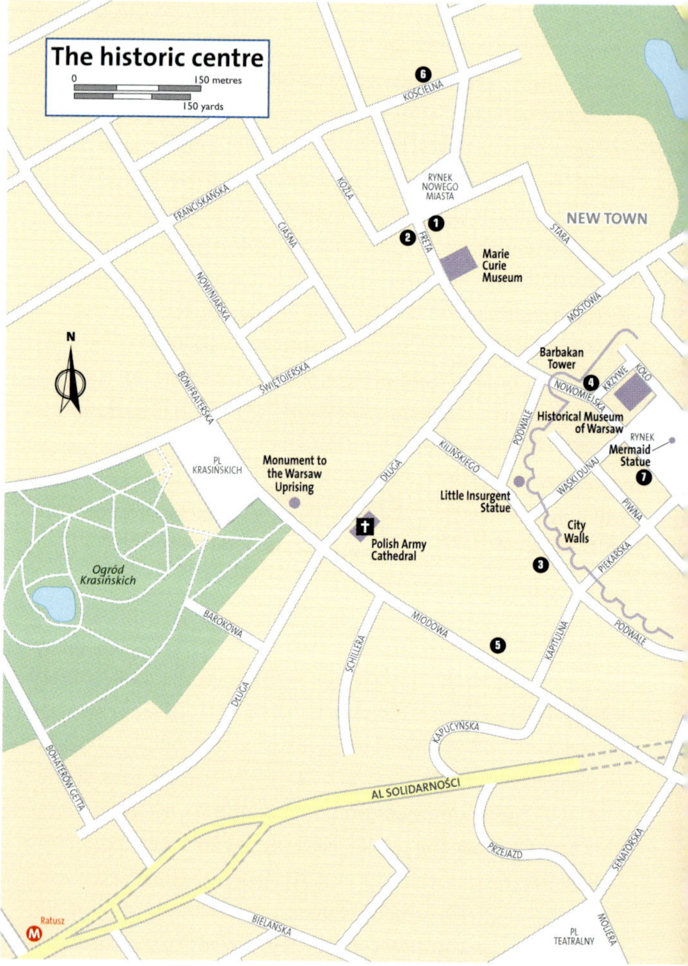
The historic centre
0
150 metres
150 yards
N
NEW TOWN
RYNEK NOWEGO MIASTA
Marie Curie Museum
Barbakan Tower
Historical Museum of Warsaw
RYNEK
Mermaid Statue
Little Insurgent Statue
City Walls
Monument to the Warsaw Uprising
Polish Army Cathedral
PL KRASIŃSKICH
Ogród Krasińskich
KOŚCIELNA
FRANCISZKAŃSKA
KOZLA
CIASNA
FRETA
STARA
MOSTOWA
NOWINIARSKA
ŚWIĘTOJERSKA
BONIFRATERSKA
NOWOMIEJSKA
KRZYWE
KOŁO
PODWALE
KILIŃSKIEGO
WĄSKI DUNAJ
PIWNA
PIEKARSKA
DŁUGA
BAROKOWA
MIODOWA
SCHILLERA
KAPITULNA
KAPUCYŃSKA
AL SOLIDARNOŚCI
BOHATERÓW GETTA
PRZEJAZD
SENATORSKA
BIELAŃSKA
MOLIERA
PL TEATRALNY
Ratusz

Citadel
Warsaw Zoo
WYBRZEŻE GDAŃSKIE
WYBRZEŻE HELSKIE
Vistula
WODNA
BUGAJ
BRZOZOWA
OLD TOWN
St John's Cathedral
KANONIA
ŚWIĘTOJAŃSKA
MOST ŚLĄSKO-DĄBROWSKI
Royal Castle
PLAC ZAMKOWY
St Sigismund's Column
WYBRZEŻE GDAŃSKIE
MARIENSZTAT
St Anne's Church
DOBRA
KRAKOWSKIE
KOZIA
BEDNARSKA
FURMAŃSKA
......Metro Stop
.........Cathedral
......Information
.............Airport
.......Railway Stn
...........Hospital

WARSAW UPRISING

With the imminent collapse of Nazi Germany and guarantees of Allied aid, Poland's wartime military movement, the Home Army, took the decision to liberate Warsaw and install an independent government before the advancing Soviets – already based on the Praga side of the river – could arrive. Co-ordinated attacks were launched on German positions across the city on 1 August 1944, with sweeping initial success; for the first time in five years the Polish flag fluttered over the city. But the news of the rising infuriated Hitler, who sent crack military units to crush the insurrection. Allied aid drops failed to make a mark, and with the Red Army based stoically on the other side of the river, the conflict became a futile street battle with Polish forces pummelled mercilessly by the full weight of the Nazi army. Faced with a hopeless situation, the Poles finally capitulated on 2 October. Remaining inhabitants were expelled, then the Germans dynamited the city. The old town area was the scene of the most brutal fighting, and the **Little Insurgent Statue** (ⓐ ul. Podwale) is dedicated to the memory of the children who died in combat. Further down on pl. Krasińskich stands the **Monument to the Warsaw Uprising**, depicting a group of soldiers escaping into the sewers below. Around Warsaw numerous plaques mark out the site of mass killings organised by the Nazis during 1944, though to appreciate the full scale of this human tragedy a visit to the **Warsaw Uprising Museum** (ⓐ ul. Przyokopowa 28) is crucial (see page 97).

town in style then hop into one of the horse-drawn carriages, or alternatively climb the tower attached to St Anne's Church (ⓐ ul. Krakowskie Przedmieście 68) for panoramic views. On your way to the Rynek (main square) don't miss the mini-sized square on ul. Kanonia. The bell resting on the ground is the original one from St John's Cathedral, glued together after shattering during World War II, while the nearby tenement at number 20/22 is allegedly the narrowest house in the world. The Rynek itself is the main magnet of the old town, however, with its central point of note being a mermaid statue;

Syrenka: the mermaid who is a symbol of the city

otherwise known as the Syrenka, it was a mermaid who allegedly guided Prince Kazimerz to safety after he got lost in the area that is now Warsaw. Surrounding the statue on all four sides is a patchwork of colourful burgher houses rebuilt following the 18th-century plans of architect Tylman van Gameren.

Royal Castle

Dating from the 14th century the castle originally served as the home of the Polish monarchy, before acting as lodgings for the president and then the seat of Parliament. Anyone who's seen the 'before and after' pictures of World War II Warsaw will know the castle was left as a pile of ruins after the Nazis made a hasty exit, and reconstruction of the castle was only completed in 1984. Today the prescribed route takes you through regal chambers dripping with gold, silver and priceless artwork, and it's difficult to imagine that this structure is actually younger than the Novotel. Of particular note are the Canaletto room, adorned with the artist's paintings of 18th-century Warsaw, the chapel containing the heart of Polish freedom fighter Tadeusz Kościuiszko, and the spectacular throne room – rebuilt using several original fragments recovered from the rubble. In the castle cellars take a look at objects discovered during archaeological excavations undertaken after 1945, bearing in mind not to stray too close to anything for fear of incurring the wrath of ever-vigilant wardens.

ⓐ pl. Zamkowy 4 ⓣ 022 657 21 70 🕒 10.00–16.00 Tues–Sat, 11.00–16.00 Sun, closed Mon

St Sigismund's Column towers above the Royal Castle

CULTURE

Historical Museum of Warsaw

Your visit to this fantastic museum begins with a film detailing the story of Warsaw's destruction in 1944 (English showings held at 12.00). After this sobering introduction the museum unfolds before you, its 60-plus rooms taking you through the history of the city, from its early beginnings to the days of martial law in 1981. Medieval city maps document the city's evolution, while elsewhere visitors can observe tapestries, oil paintings, archaeological finds and clothing, all under the watchful gaze of fierce-looking curators who loom with intent.
ⓐ Rynek Starego Miasta 42 ⓣ 022 635 16 25 ⓛ 11.00–18.00 Tues & Thur, 10.00–15.30 Wed & Fri, 10.30–16.30 Sat & Sun, closed Mon. Admission charge

Marie Curie Museum

A rather lacklustre affair celebrating the life and work of one of Poland's – and possibly the world's – most celebrated women. Born Maria Skłodowska in Warsaw on 7 November 1867, the two-times Nobel-winning scientist's very own museum is a small and decidedly musty thing, with just two diminutive rooms of displays including personal effects, letters, odd-looking scientific devices and a model of a nuclear power plant. A small leaflet is available in English to make the visit just that little more worthwhile, but really this is a bit of an underachievement.
ⓐ ul. Freta 16 ⓣ 022 831 80 92 ⓛ 09.30–16.00 Wed–Fri, 08.30–16.00 Tues, 10.00–16.00 Sat, 10.00–15.00 Sun, closed Mon. Admission charge

Polish Army Cathedral

Consecrated in 1701, this cathedral has, through the ages, served as a prison, an orphanage, a depot for German soldiers during World War I and even an Orthodox church during Imperial Russian rule, complete with the obligatory onion domes. Used as an observation point and a field hospital by Polish forces during the Warsaw Uprising, the building was repeatedly targeted by the Luftwaffe, and suffered the same fiery fate as the other buildings in this area. Its reconstruction was completed in 1960 following original architect's sketches from the 17th century. Its entrance houses numerous paintings depicting Polish military moments, and the names of 15,000 Polish officers murdered by the NKVD in the Katyń massacre of 1940 are inscribed on plaques in the chapel near the altar.

ⓐ ul. Długa 13/15

St John's Cathedral

Dating from the 14th century, Warsaw's oldest place of worship was obliterated in 1944 and rebuilt in Gothic style in the post-war years. The tracks of a Goliath – a German remote-controlled tank used to devastating effect during the Warsaw Uprising – hang from one of the outside walls in memory of the brutality this cathedral witnessed. As in the old town around it, the rebuilding work undertaken has been outstanding, and the interiors are decorated with the works of Wit Stwosz, best known for his magnificent altarpiece in Kraków's St Mary's Basilica. Poland's last monarch, Stanisław August Poniatowski, declared his historic constitution of 1791

St John's Cathedral

inside this remarkable edifice, and it was also the sight of his coronation. His body now lies in the crypt alongside cultural luminaries such as the writer Henryk Sienkiewicz and the former presidents Gabriel Narutowicz and Ignacy Jan Paderewski.

ⓐ ul. Świetojańska 8 ⓣ 022 831 02 89 ⓛ 10.00–13.00, 15.00–17.30 Mon–Sat, 15.00–17.30 Sun

RETAIL THERAPY

If you're looking for Japanese gadgetry, you're in the wrong place. Shopping in Warsaw's historic quarter means a choice of two things: either scabby little places selling overpriced tourist trinkets, or top-quality establishments selling overpriced antiques. Spending in the old town usually means overspending in the old town; watch a foreigner enter a shop in the old town and hear the cash bells ring. You will find better deals in the city centre, but that's not to say the antique stores lining the old town's cobbled streets aren't worth exploring. This is a collector's paradise with several shops specialising in everything from pre-war stamps to period furniture. If you've done your background reading you will already be aware that Poland is a major source of amber, and you'll find numerous stores in the old town focused on this commodity. When buying amber here, bear in mind that it can be easily re-melted and re-shaped; if it looks too perfect, then the chances are it probably has been.

TAKING A BREAK

Belle Epoque £ ❶ Belle Epoque is a refuge from the 21st century and not unlike stepping back in time. Enjoy tea and cakes while sitting amid dusty gramophones, globes and grandfather clocks. Doubling as an antique shop, everything in here could be yours in return for a large number of coins. ⓐ ul. Freta 18 ⓣ 022 635 41 05 ⓛ 13.00–23.00 Mon–Sat, closed Sun

Pod Samsonem £ ❷ One of the few Jewish-themed eateries in town, and a bit of a let-down. Service inside this basic-looking restaurant is virtually non-existent, while the plates of (non-kosher certified) Jewish/Polish food have a tendency to disappoint. On the plus side this is one of the few places in the old town that does not assume all tourists earn rockstar wages, so if nothing else it's not a bad venue to regroup after a day spent trolling the local museums. ⓐ ul. Freta 3/5 ⓣ 022 831 17 88 ⓛ 10.00–23.00 Mon–Sat, closed Sun

Podwale Kompania Piwna £ ❸ Accessed via a faux Bavarian courtyard, this is the ideal introduction to local dining. A series of chambers are filled with stout timber fittings while live bands stalk from room to room playing traditional oompah noises. Served on wooden platters and steel pans the portions here are enormous, with grilled animals of all descriptions accompanied by heaps of cabbage. Advanced bookings recommended in evenings. ⓐ ul. Podwale 25 ⓣ 022 635 63 14 ⓦ www.podwale25.pl ⓛ 11.00–01.00 Tues–Sat, 14.00–01.00 Mon, 12.00–01.00 Sun

Same Fusy £ ❹ A subterranean café where the mystical Eastern décor induces a zen-like calm on all who visit. The menu includes a choice of more than 100 teas, with flavours including baffling choices like Winnie the Pooh. ⓐ ul. Nowomiejska 10 ⓣ 022 635 90 14 ⓛ 11.00–23.00 Mon–Sun

Honoratka ££ ❺ Breathe the history of centuries past inside what was formerly the haunt of local-born composer Fryderyk Chopin. Animal skins adorn the vaulted interiors while the summer garden proves an oasis of tranquillity, and the ideal spot for a cold refreshment while poring over your collection of maps. On the menu are meat-heavy local delicacies such as goose and wild boar. ⓐ ul. Miodowa 14 ⓣ 022 635 03 97 ⓦ www.oberzanamiodowej.pl ⓛ 11.00–22.00 Mon–Sun

La Rotisserie £££ ❻ A complete indulgence, but guaranteed to leave an impact on your better half. Unsurprisingly Warsaw's best hotel is complemented by an equally impressive restaurant. A chic interior is matched by beautifully presented dishes influenced by Polish and French cooking. ⓐ ul. Kościelna 12 (Le Regina Hotel) ⓣ 022 531 60 70 ⓦ www.leregina.com ⓛ 12.00–23.00 Mon–Sat, 13.00–22.00 Sun

U Fukiera £££ ❼ Poland's most famous restaurant, with a guestbook that contains names like Schiffer, Deneuve and Chirac. Naturally you're expected to pay exorbitant prices, so bring a suitcase filled with notes if you wish to avoid dish-duty in the kitchen. The results are well worth the outlay, with inventive game dishes served inside a set of decadent rooms that bring to mind an aristocratic residence. Ideal for a last-night splurge. ⓐ Rynek Starego Miasto 27 ⓣ 022 831 10 13 ⓦ www.ufukiera.pl ◷ 12.00–23.00 daily

AFTER DARK

Tomba Tomba Weirdos, deviants and freaks can't keep away from Tomba Tomba and this rates as one of Warsaw's most permissive clubs. Spread across four levels, this converted townhouse features a whirlpool and a king-size bed, both of which witness plenty of monkey business come the weekend. You'll find some of the capital's top house DJs taking to the decks, keeping the metrosexual crowd gurning until daybreak. ⓐ ul. Brzozowa 37 ⓣ 022 831 95 39 ◷ 22.00–12.00 Fri & Sat, 21.00–04.00 Sun, closed Mon–Thur

Jazz Bistro An atmospheric jazz venue with vaulted ceilings, a glass-covered atrium and expert bartenders elaborately fixing the poison of your choice. Live performances take place most evenings, making this an ideal venue to practise the art of seduction. ⓐ ul. Piwna 40 ⓣ 022 887 87 64 ⓦ www.jazzbistro.pl ◷ 10.00–23.00 Sun–Thur, 10.00–24.00 Fri & Sat

John Bull A reminder of what a British pub looked like before the brewing industry was hijacked by alcopops and gastro-pubs. Patterned carpets and framed pics of landed gentry hunting animals occupy every conceivable space, and it appears largely overlooked by Warsaw's legions of expats – which is by no means a bad thing. In summer, repair to the terrace to admire views of the River Vistula. ⓐ ul. Jezuicka 4 ⓣ 022 831 03 67 ⓛ 11.00–23.00 Mon–Sun

The Ghetto Heroes Monument commemorates the 1943 uprising

The city centre

While the old town is beautiful to look at, it soon transpires that no one actually lives there. To find Warsaw's beating heart you'll need the city centre, a chaotic mix of daring skyscrapers, dilapidated tower blocks and art nouveau structures that somehow made it through the war. The jigsaw of styles and the frenetic pace of street life bring to mind the Berlin of the 90s and it's hard not to embrace the addictive energy that the centre exhales. You'll spot taxis at every turn, though, even if you're not wearing financial shackles, the quickest and most efficient method of traversing this vast area is by using the excellent public transport network.

Monument to Chopin in Łazienki Park

JEWISH WARSAW

Until World War II Warsaw was home to the world's largest Jewish population outside of New York, with approximately 350,000 Jews registered as living in the city at the outbreak of the war. The creation of the Ghetto in 1940 signalled the beginning of the end for Warsaw's Jews, with more than 300,000 eventually perishing in the gas chambers of Treblinka. The final days of the Ghetto were marked by the Warsaw Ghetto Uprising; often confused with the Warsaw Uprising, this equally heroic chapter of Warsaw's history saw poorly armed Jewish resistance fighters take on the German forces in a battle that lasted from 18 January till 23 April 1943. With the Ghetto retaken the Nazis set about razing it to the ground, erasing all traces of their horrific crimes. As such, sights of interest are few and often very far between. Catch a glimpse of a surviving piece of the Ghetto wall at ⓐ ul Sienna 55; the courtyard where you'll find this moving piece of modern history is usually locked, but don't be shy in ringing door buzzers to gain access. An ugly monument on ⓐ ul. Stawki marks the site of the Umschlagplatz, the loading platform where Jews were packed into cattle trucks bound for Treblinka, while the nearby park on ⓐ ul. Zamenhofa contains a monument in honour of the Ghetto Uprising. The stone cladding on the monument was originally earmarked to build a Nazi victory arch. To find out more about Jewish life in Warsaw, pencil in a visit to the Jewish Historical Institute (see page 83)

The city centre
0
500 metres
0
500 yards
Powązki Cemetery
Umschlagplatz Memorial
Pawiak Prison
Ghetto Uprising Memorial
Ogród Krasińskich
Jewish Historical Institute
Ratusz
Ogród Saski
Świętokrzyska
Palace of Culture & Science
CITY CENTRE
WOLA
OCHOTA
Centralna
Wkd
Ochota
Glowna
Zachodnia
PLAC ZAWISZY
DZIKA
STAWKI
NISKA
DUBOIS
MIŁA
LEWARTOWSKIEGO
KARMELICKA
ZAMENHOFA
GEN ANDERSA
WAŁOWA
FRANCISZKAŃSKA
BONIFRATERSKA
ŚWIĘTOJERSKA
DŁUGA
SMOCZA
ESPERANTO
ANIELEWICZA
AL JANA PAWŁA II
PAWIA
DZIELNA
NOWOLIPKI
NOWOLIPIE
TŁOMACKIE
OKOPOWA
OBOZOWA
GIBALSKIEGO
AL SOLIDARNOŚCI
ORLA
ELEKTORALNA
PLASIA
WOLNOŚĆ
KACZA
ŻYTNIA
LESZNO
OGRODOWE
ŻELAZNA
CIEPŁA
PŁOCKA
DŁUGOSZA
TYSZKIEWICZA
MŁYNARSKA
KAROLKOWA
GÓRCZEWSKA
WAWELBERGA
ŚLĄSZICA
KROCHMALNA
WALICÓW
GRZYBOWSKA
PRÓŻNA
WOLSKA
CHŁODNA
KOTLARSKA
JAKTOROWSKA
TOWAROWA
WRONIA
PERECA
TWARDA
ŚWIĘTOKRZYSKA
SKIERNIEWICKA
SIEDMIOGRODZKA
PRZYOKOPOWA
ŁUCKA
PROSTA
PAŃSKA
SIENNA
SILSKA
EMILII PLATER
MIEDZIANA
ZŁOTA
KASPRZAKA
CHMIELNA
AL JEROZOLIMSKIE
SZARYCH SZEREGÓW
BRYLOWSKA
SREBRNA
KOLEJOWA
CHAŁUBIŃSKIEGO
NOWOGRODZKA
LINDLEYA
OCZKI
HOŻA
PRĄDZYŃSKIEGO
KOSZYKOWA
SPISKA
GRÓJECKA
RASZYŃSKA
TUNELOWA
KRZYWICKIEGO
NOWOWIEJSKA
SĘKOCIŃSKA
SŁUPECKA
BARSKA
KALISKA
FILTROWA
AL NIEPODLEGŁOŚCI
GRZYMAŁY
SZCZĘŚLIWICKA
BIAŁOBRZESKA
KOPIŃSKA
MOCHNACKIEGO
REJA
WAWELSKA
3
5
6

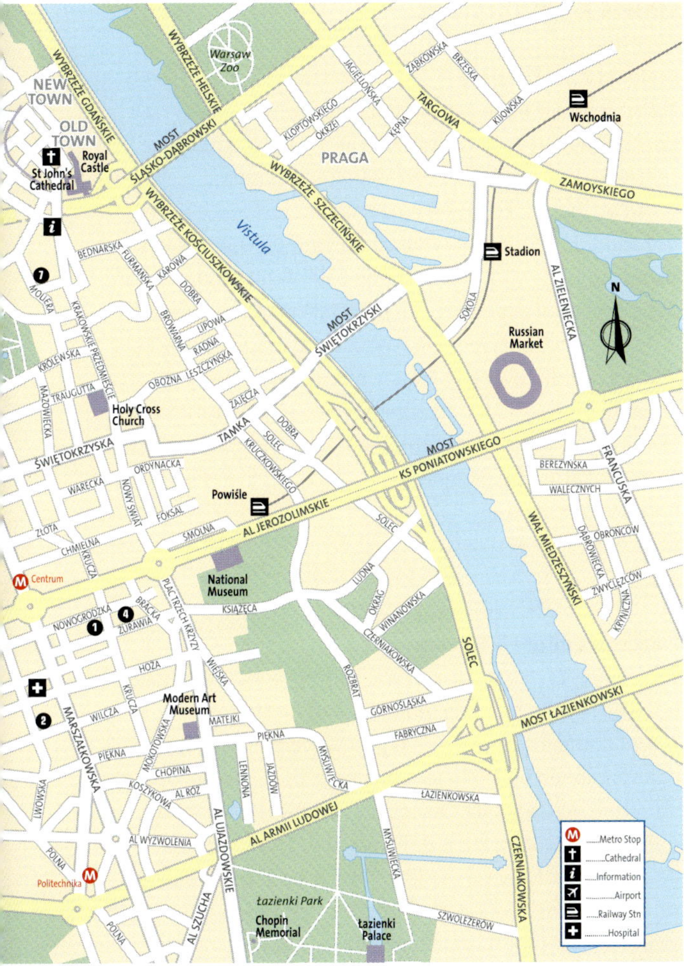
NEW TOWN
OLD TOWN
Royal Castle
St John's Cathedral
Warsaw Zoo
WYBRZEŻE GDAŃSKIE
WYBRZEŻE HELSKIE
MOST ŚLĄSKO-DĄBROWSKI
WYBRZEŻE KOŚCIUSZKOWSKIE
WYBRZEŻE SZCZECIŃSKIE
Vistula
PRAGA
JAGIELLOŃSKA
KŁOPTOWSKIEGO
OKRZEI
KĘPNA
ZĄBKOWSKA
BRZESKA
TARGOWA
KIJOWSKA
Wschodnia
ZAMOYSKIEGO
Stadion
AL ZIELENIECKA
SOKOLA
Russian Market
N
BEDNARSKA
FURMAŃSKA
KAROWA
DOBRA
BROWARNA
LIPOWA
RADNA
OBOZNA
LESZCZYŃSKA
MOLIERA
KRAKOWSKIE PRZEDMIEŚCIE
KRÓLEWSKA
MAZOWIECKA
TRAUGUTTA
Holy Cross Church
ZAJĘCZA
TAMKA
SOLEC
KRUCZKOWSKIEGO
MOST ŚWIĘTOKRZYSKI
MOST KS PONIATOWSKIEGO
ŚWIĘTOKRZYSKA
ORDYNACKA
WARECKA
NOWY ŚWIAT
FOKSAL
Powiśle
AL JEROZOLIMSKIE
SMOLNA
ZŁOTA
CHMIELNA
KRUCZA
Centrum
National Museum
PLAC TRZECH KRZYŻY
BRACKA
NOWOGRODZKA
ŻURAWIA
KSIĄŻĘCA
LUDNA
OKRĄG
WINANOWSKA
CZERNIAKOWSKA
BEREZYŃSKA
WALECZNYCH
FRANCUSKA
DĄBROWIECKA
OBROŃCÓW
ZWYCIĘZCÓW
KRYNICZNA
WAŁ MIEDZESZYŃSKI
SOLEC
HOŻA
WIEJSKA
ROZBRAT
GÓRNOŚLĄSKA
FABRYCZNA
MOST ŁAZIENKOWSKI
Modern Art Museum
MATEJKI
WILCZA
MARSZAŁKOWSKA
PIĘKNA
MOKOTOWSKA
CHOPINA
KOSZYKOWA
AL RÓŻ
LENNONA
JAZDÓW
MYŚLIWIECKA
ŁAZIENKOWSKA
AL ARMII LUDOWEJ
AL UJAZDOWSKIE
LWOWSKA
AL WYZWOLENIA
POLNA
Politechnika
AL SZUCHA
Łazienki Park
Chopin Memorial
Łazienki Palace
SZWOLEŻERÓW
CZERNIAKOWSKA
Metro Stop
Cathedral
Information
Airport
Railway Stn
Hospital

SIGHTS & ATTRACTIONS

Łazienki Park & Palace

For a breath of fresh air visit Warsaw's most popular park, an 80-ha (198-acre) site established in the 17th century. Its centrepiece is the Palace on the Water, a classic structure built on an artificial lake, and the permanent residence of Poland's last monarch, Stanisław August Poniatowski. Sightseers can snoop around living quarters and ballrooms, though for the definitive local experience an exploration of the palace grounds is necessary. Amid weeping willows and majestic peacocks visitors can discover the Temple of Diana (erected in 1822), a monument to Chopin, an orangery housing a formidably expensive restaurant, botanical gardens and even a classicist amphitheatre. The gardens are also host to live concerts each Sunday evening over the summer.

ⓐ ul. Agrykola 1 ⓣ 022 621 62 41 ⓦ www.lazienki-krolewskie.pl
ⓑ 09.00–16.00 Tues–Sun, closed Mon

Palace of Culture & Science

You couldn't miss this one if you tried; soaring 231 m (758 ft) into the sky the building remains the tallest in Poland, despite recent competition from its high-rise neighbours. Originally commissioned by Stalin as a 'gift from the Soviet people' the structure actually takes its inspiration from the capitalist world, namely the Empire State Building. Stalin had sent a secret delegation to New York to learn about both the building and American construction methods, though the outbreak of World War II meant that it wasn't until 1952 that his architects were to begin putting their knowledge into practice. Lev Rudynev was put in charge of the design, and set about making the building into one of the most notorious examples of Socialist Realist architecture in the world. Built using an estimated 40 million bricks and housing 3,288 rooms, the Palace's purpose was to serve as not just party headquarters but also 'the people's castle', with invitations to the annual New Year's Eve Ball issued to the best workers in socialist Poland.

Once inside, the ground floor becomes a maze of halls and corridors; brass chandeliers hang over clacking parquet flooring and allegorical socialist reliefs take inspiration from ancient

The Palace of Culture and Science, a gift from the Soviet people

mythology – it's easy to imagine Bond sneaking around planting listening devices. Although Stalin never made it to the Palace, Comrade Brezhnev did, and nowadays it's possible to view the room he used before famously staggering to address the crowd gathered in the blood-red Congress Hall. The viewing platform on the 30th floor offers panoramic views of the city spinning below you. If you're looking for further examples of the Socialist Realist style then a visit to pl. Konstytcuji is required. Christened in 1952, the square was to serve as the focal point for state parades and today its monumental street lamps and reliefs depicting square-jawed farmers and miners sit juxtaposed with fast-food empires and electronics stores.

ⓐ pl. Defilad 1 ⓣ 022 656 76 00 ⓦ www.pkin.pl ⓛ 09.00–18.00 Tues–Sat, 10.00–17.00 Sun, closed Mon

CULTURE

Holy Cross Church

Originally built around 1696 and standing on the site of a former church destroyed during the Swedish Deluge of the mid-17th century, like so many churches and fine buildings in Warsaw, the truly spectacular beauty you see today actually dates from just a couple of generations ago, having been well and truly flattened during World War II. One of Warsaw's best examples of baroque architecture, the inside of this enormous beast is overflowing with golden altars and other spectacular sights. Perhaps its most famous addition is that of Chopin's heart, found inside one of the church's huge supporting columns.

ⓐ ul. Krakowskie Przedmieście 3 ⓣ 022 826 89 10

Jewish Historical Institute

A really well-presented evocation of past Jewish religious and secular life in Warsaw and Poland in general, opened in 1948, this highly commendable achievement is Poland's only institution dedicated entirely to the study of the history and culture of Polish Jewry. Tracing Jewish life in the country from its beginnings up until the Holocaust, exhibitions include some extraordinary photographs, salvaged religious artefacts and a small cinema showing disturbing footage of life in the Warsaw Ghetto.

ⓐ ul. Tłomackie 3/5 ⓣ 022 827 92 21 ⓛ 09.00–16.00 Mon–Wed & Fri, 11.00–18.00 Thur, closed Sat & Sun. Admission charge

Holy Cross Church

Modern Art Museum

An 18th-century baroque castle is a rather unlikely setting for a contemporary art gallery, but inside you'll find a wonderful series of displays showcasing the best in Polish contemporary art, with a particular leaning towards the most baffling and often silly types.
ⓐ al. Ujazdowskie 6 ⓣ 022 628 12 71 ⓛ 11.00–19.00 Tues–Thur, Sat & Sun, 11.00–21.00 Fri, closed Mon. Admission charge

National Museum

A world-class collection inside a grotesque lump of concrete, exhibits include some breathtaking examples of 15th-century Flemish painting and tapestries, artefacts from ancient Egypt and a vast array of Polish treasures from furniture to 19th-century Polish paintings. Highlights include works from the leading 20th-century Polish masters, including Witkiewicz and Szczepkowski. A must-see for anyone visiting the city.
ⓐ al. Jerozolimskie 3 ⓣ 022 621 10 31 ⓛ 10.00–16.00 Tues & Wed, Fri–Sun, 10.00–18.00 Thur, closed Mon. Admission charge

Pawiak Prison

More depressing wartime associations are to be found in the reconstructed basement of this once-Tsarist prison. Commandeered by the Nazis, Pawiak was used as a political prison and its gloomy cells and displays of personal belongings leave a dark mark on the day. Some 37,000 people were executed here, and a further 60,000 shipped off to death camps.
ⓐ ul. Dzielna 24/26 ⓣ 022 831 92 89 ⓛ 09.00–16.00 Thur & Sat, 09.00–17.00 Wed, 10.00–17.00 Fri, 10.00–16.00 Sun, closed Mon & Tues

RETAIL THERAPY

While the natives flock to the out-of-town malls, visitors will be pleased to know there is little reason to do so; all you wish for can be found in the city centre. **Nowy Świat** is regarded as the principal shopping artery with boutiques and antique stores lining the street, though to hit the really exclusive end of Warsaw shopping follow Nowy Świat down to **pl. Trzech Krzyży**. It's here you'll find the big-buck designer clothes stores. If you're curious to know what the great big glass bubble by the train station is, that's the **Złote Tarasy shopping centre**: an inner-city mall containing an entertainment complex, Poland's only Hard Rock Café and the usual slew of high-street retailers.

TAKING A BREAK

Namaste £ ❶ Easy to miss, so rely on your nose to guide you into this tiny hole-in-the-wall enterprise. This is the best Indian food in the country, so it comes as a surprise that it isn't even a proper restaurant – more an Indian grocery store with two wobbly tables set aside for diners. The menu isn't extensive but the chefs labouring in the background are masters of their craft and can be relied on to deliver knockout curries that leave the locals with blistered mouths. If all the seats are occupied then do as the expats do and get your food bagged up to go.
ⓐ ul. Nowogrodzka 15 ⓣ 022 357 09 39 ⓦ www.namasteindia.pl
🕒 11.00–21.00 Mon–Sat, closed Sun

Warsaw Tortilla Factory £ ❷ Tequila girls ferry top-quality burritos and quesadillas inside this atmospheric expat fortress. Portions verge on the obscene while the mango habanero sauce carries a nuclear bite that's proved the undoing of many a good man. As night falls, the Tortilla Factory transforms into a popular drinking den, with the L-shaped bar area becoming besieged by foreign accents. ⓐ ul. Wilcza 46 (enter from ul. Poznańka) ⓣ 022 621 86 22 ⓛ 12.00–23.00 daily

Atrio ££ ❸ A seriously impressive restaurant situated in the heart of Warsaw's financial quarter. By day it's all beeping phones and hushed voices as the corporate set talk conspiratorially about mergers and percentages, though by night Atrio breathes out and transforms into a slick, romantic restaurant. The food is modern international and rates as one of the best meals you'll find, while the prices are not as prohibitive as the designer surroundings would suggest. ⓐ al. Jana Pawła II 23 ⓣ 022 653 96 00 ⓦ www.atrio.waw.pl ⓛ 08.00–24.00 daily

Café 6/12 ££ ❹ Treading the line between restaurant, café and bar, 6/12 offers a creative menu, as well as some of the only bagels to be discovered in Warsaw. Set inside a cavernous Socialist Realist building, the design is stark and urban, softened by moody lighting and ambient background noise, while the crowd could well apply to be extras in *Sex and the City*. ⓐ ul. Żurawia 6/12 ⓣ 022 622 53 33 ⓛ 08.00–23.00 Mon–Thur, 08.00–24.00 Fri, 10.00–24.00 Sat, 10.00–23.00 Sun

Folk Gospoda ££ ❺ If you're looking for the signature Polish eating experience you could do a lot worse than this rustic-themed eatery, where high-cal servings of farm animals come piled on huge plates. Traditional live din completes your immersion into rural Poland. ⓐ ul. Waliców 13 ⓣ 022 890 16 05 ⓦ www.folkgospoda.pl ⓛ 08.00–23.00 Mon–Fri, 10.30–23.00 Sat & Sun

Jimmy Bradley's ££ ❻ An unappealing location on the ground floor of an office block should not detract from what transpires to be Warsaw's homeliest boozer. Landlord Kevin has a history of running bars and his brand of Irish hospitality has earned Bradley's a loyal following. Decorated with stained glass and framed rugby shirts, this pub touts the atmosphere of your local back home, complete with a TV tuned into Sky Sports, and the distant thump of darts missing their target. Prepare yourself for the carnage ahead with their traditional Irish breakfast. ⓐ ul. Sienna 39 ⓣ 022 654 66 56 ⓦ www.bradleys.pl ⓛ 10.00–01.00 Mon–Thur, 10.00–02.00 Fri, 12.00–02.00 Sat & Sun

Sakana ££ ❼ Warsaw's fashionista love sushi, and the clamour to please the young rich has led to a slew of sushi stops springing up. If you only concern yourself with the best then you'll need to put Sakana in your crosshairs; expertly prepared raw fish floats by on tiny boats while staff wearing Mr Miyagi headgear cut up your lunch from behind a central bar. ⓐ ul. Moliera 4/6 ⓣ 022 826 59 58 ⓦ www.sushibar.pl ⓛ 12.00–23.00 Mon–Sat, 13.00–22.00 Sun

AFTER DARK

Bars & clubs

Bar Below In spite of the stark and urban design, Irish landlord Niall has managed to re-create the warming atmosphere of your local bar. Trade banter with the regulars at the bar or take to the lounge area to watch Sky Sports. The menu excels itself too. ⓐ ul. Marszałkowska 64 ⓣ 022 621 18 50 ⓛ 12.00–24.00 Sun–Wed, 12.00–03.00 Thur–Sat

BrowArmia This is a jewel of a microbrewery displaying all the requisite vats and dials. A great primer for bar crawls following the Krakowskie Przedmieśćie/Nowy Świat trail, with sturdy bar food available. ⓐ ul. Królewska 1 ⓣ 022 826 54 55 ⓦ www.browarmia.pl ⓛ 12.00–24.00 Mon–Sat, closed Sun

Klubo Kawiarnia If you manage to get past the door police, this is one of the premier nightspots in town; for men, a retro football top and a record bag are usually enough to gain entrance; for women, a plastic smile will suffice. What space isn't filled with vintage commie memorabilia is taken up with junkstore lampshades and armchairs, while spaced-out clubbers try daring moves to house and funk accompaniments. ⓐ ul. Czackiego (first gate from ul. Świętokrzyska) ⓛ 20.00–03.00 Mon–Thur, 20.00–06.00 Fri & Sat, closed Sun

Luzztro There is no better place in Poland to blast your brain with techno sounds. You'll find Luzztro lying through a reflective doorway behind which people party till the blurry hours. No design gimmicks here, if anything this club is seriously grotty; the draw is the music, with imported DJs playing cutting-edge sounds. a al. Jerozolimskie 6 w www.luztro.pl 21.00–06.00 Tues–Thur, open around the clock from Friday 21.00 till Monday 06.00

NoBo Warsaw's first lounge bar and definitely still its best, though don't be surprised to be refused entry at the weekend on account of a private party. The decadent interior is filled with scarlet colours, slash screens and luxurious ottomans, and the fusion menu warrants praise. a ul. Wilcza 58a t 022 622 40 07 w www.nobobar.pl 12.00–02.00 Mon–Thur, 12.00–05.00 Fri, 18.00–05.00 Sat, closed Sun

Sense This cleverly designed spot continues to act as a benchmark for all new bars. Either opt to sit in the restaurant section where a list of fusion delights await, or take to the crushed-glass bar to test some of Poland's most potent cocktail concoctions. a ul. Nowy Świat 19 t 022 826 65 70 w www.sensecafe.com 12.00–23.00 Mon–Thur, 12.00–00.30 Fri & Sat, 12.00–22.00 Sun

Milch A design masterpiece with superb booth seating and a VIP room kitted out with expensive installations and a bar that is 25 per cent more expensive. This is the hottest address in town when it comes to spotting celebs, and the list of guest DJs is second to none. In spite of this Milch has no dance floor, leading to lots of dancing people invading your space with stray elbows. a ul. Hoża 50 t 022 745 05 60 21.00–04.00 Mon–Sat, closed Sun

Out of the centre

Warsaw's spread-out nature and gridlocked streets make it all the more tempting for visitors to limit themselves to the city centre, though doing so often means missing the city's true glories. While much of the area that wraps the city centre is a no-man's-land of post-war tower blocks, areas such as Praga are enjoying a much-publicised social revival, while districts like Wilanów have drawn comparisons to Versailles – and for good reason.

SIGHTS & ATTRACTIONS

Powązki Cemetery

A beguiling cemetery originally founded in 1790 at a time when inner-city cemeteries were being closed down on sanitary grounds. Some supreme examples of sepulchral art are to be

Unusual gravestone, Powązki Cemetery

found in this vast area, with those interred including the hardcore Stalinist Bolesław Bierut, director Krysztof Kieślowski and the aviators Żwirko and Wigura. Don't miss the Jewish cemetery next door, a haunting space that's home to more than 250,000 tombs, many of which are overgrown and sinking: a poignant epitaph to the area's Jewish past.

ⓐ ul. Powązkowska 14 ⓣ 022 633 21 40 ◷ 08.00 till dusk

Praga

Found at the start of Warsaw's Monopoly board, the Praga district on the right-hand side of the River Vistula has traditionally enjoyed a reputation as home to the city's criminal pondlife. Undestroyed during World War II, the battered riverside dwellings offer a convincing trip back in time, so much so that Roman Polański chose to shoot several scenes of his Ghetto epic *The Pianist* here. Praga was spared the fate of the rest of Warsaw in 1944 on account of it already being occupied by Soviet forces. This is where the Red Army's advance came to a halt while the Warsaw Uprising raged on the other side of the river – the rusting Soviet War Memorial standing on the intersection of Targowa and al. Solidarnośći remains one of the most unloved and neglected monuments in the city.

Today the bullet-bitten tenement buildings are seeing a new lease of life as they become colonised by local art groups and the area now finds itself touted as Poland's equivalent to London's Soho. Oddities abound, from the sad-looking bears who can be found living on a concrete island next to Praski Park, to the overgrown Jewish cemetery – the oldest in the city – found on the corner of Św. Wincentego and ul. Odrowąża.

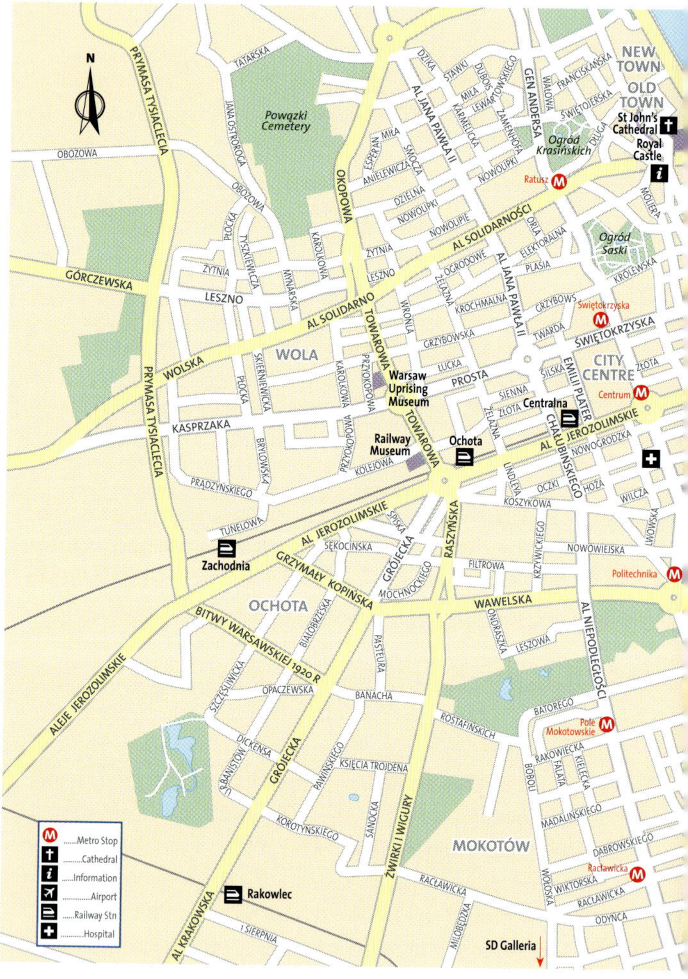
N
PRYMASA TYSIĄCLECIA
TATARSKA
JANA OSTRORÓGA
Powązki Cemetery
OBOZOWA
OKOPOWA
DZIKA
STAWKI
DUBOIS
LEWARTOWSKIEGO
AL JANA PAWŁA II
MIŁA
KARMELICKA
ZAMENHOFA
GEN ANDERSA
WAŁOWA
FRANCISZKAŃSKA
ŚWIĘTOJERSKA
NEW TOWN
OLD TOWN
St John's Cathedral
Royal Castle
Ogród Krasińskich
DŁUGA
ESPERANTO
ANIELEWICZA
SMOCZA
DZIELNA
NOWOLIPKI
NOWOLIPIE
Ratusz
MOLIERA
AL SOLIDARNOŚCI
ORLA
ELEKTORALNA
Ogród Saski
KRÓLEWSKA
PŁOCKA
TYSZKIEWICZA
KAROLKOWA
ŻYTNIA
LESZNO
GÓRCZEWSKA
MŁYNARSKA
OGRODOWE
ŻELAZNA
PLAŚNA
KROCHMALNA
GRZYBOWSKA
Świętokrzyska
ŚWIĘTOKRZYSKA
AL SOLIDARNOŚCI
TOWAROWA
WRONIA
TWARDA
WOLA
WOLSKA
SKIERNIEWICKA
PRZYOKOPOWA
Warsaw Uprising Museum
ŁUCKA
PROSTA
SIENNA
ZŁOTA
SIENNA
EMILII PLATER
CITY CENTRE
ZŁOTA
Centrum
Centralna
KASPRZAKA
BRYLOWSKA
PRZYOKOPOWA
Railway Museum
KOLEJOWA
Ochota
AL JEROZOLIMSKIE
CHAŁUBIŃSKIEGO
NOWOGRODZKA
PRĄDZYŃSKIEGO
LINDLEYA
OCZKI
HOŻA
KOSZYKOWA
WILCZA
TUNELOWA
SPISKA
LWOWSKA
Zachodnia
AL JEROZOLIMSKIE
SĘKOCIŃSKA
GRÓJECKA
RASZYŃSKA
KRZYWICKIEGO
NOWOWIEJSKA
FILTROWA
Politechnika
GRZYMAŁY KOPIŃSKA
MOCHNACKIEGO
WAWELSKA
OCHOTA
BIAŁOBRZESKA
AL NIEPODLEGŁOŚCI
ONDRASZKA
LESZOWA
BITWY WARSAWSKIEJ 1920 R
ALEJE JEROZOLIMSKIE
SZCZĘŚLIWICKA
OPACZEWSKA
BANACHA
PASTEURA
BATOREGO
ROSTAFIŃSKICH
Pole Mokotowskie
DICKENSA
RAKOWIECKA
KIELECKA
FALATA
BOBOLI
URBANISTÓW
GRÓJECKA
PAWIŃSKIEGO
KSIĘCIA TROJDENA
SANOCKA
ŻWIRKI I WIGURY
MADALIŃSKIEGO
KOROTYŃSKIEGO
MOKOTÓW
DĄBROWSKIEGO
Racławicka
WOŁOSKA
WIKTORSKA
RACŁAWICKA
RACŁAWICKA
ODYŃCA
AL KRAKOWSKA
Rakowlec
1 SIERPNIA
MIŁOBĘDZKA
SD Galleria
Metro Stop
Cathedral
Information
Airport
Railway Stn
Hospital

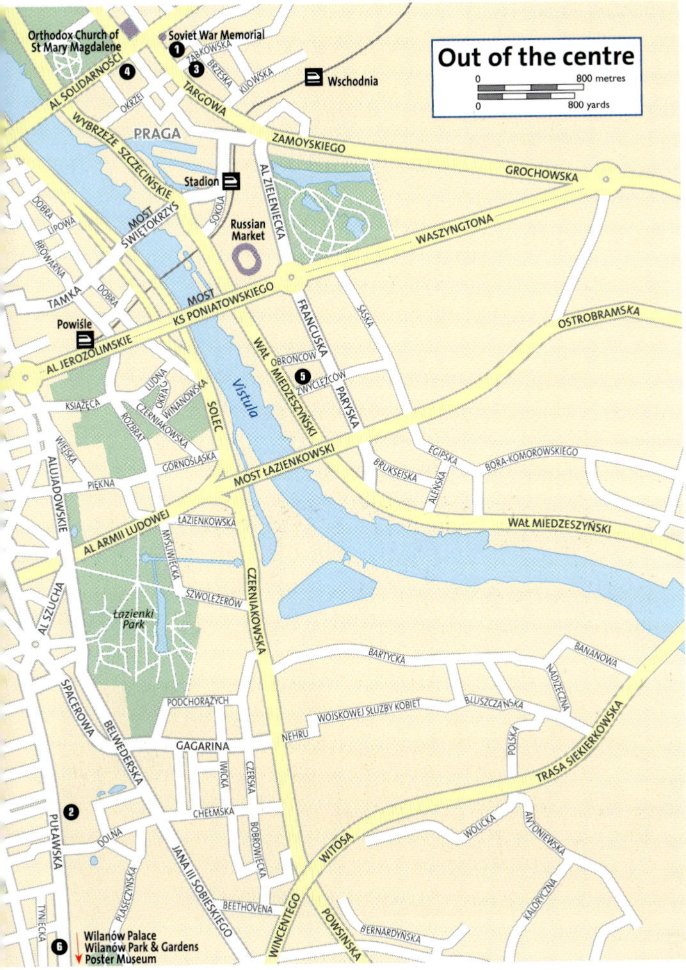
Out of the centre
0
800 metres
0
800 yards
Orthodox Church of St Mary Magdalene
Soviet War Memorial
ZĄBKOWSKA
BRZESKA
KIJOWSKA
Wschodnia
AL SOLIDARNOŚCI
TARGOWA
OKRZEI
PRAGA
WYBRZEŻE SZCZECIŃSKIE
ZAMOYSKIEGO
GROCHOWSKA
Stadion
AL ZIELENIECKA
SOKOLA
Russian Market
MOST ŚWIĘTOKRZYSKI
DOBRA
LIPOWA
BROWARNA
WASZYNGTONA
TAMKA
MOST KS PONIATOWSKIEGO
SASKA
FRANCUSKA
Powiśle
AL JEROZOLIMSKIE
OSTROBRAMSKA
WAŁ MIEDZESZYŃSKI
OBRONCÓW
ZWYCIĘZCÓW
PARYSKA
Vistula
LUDNA
OKRĄG
WINANOWSKA
CZERNIAKOWSKA
SOLEC
KSIĄŻĘCA
ROZBRAT
WIEJSKA
GÓRNOŚLĄSKA
MOST ŁAZIENKOWSKI
EGIPSKA
BRUKSELSKA
ALEŃSKA
BORA-KOMOROWSKIEGO
ALUJADOWSKIE
PIĘKNA
AL ARMII LUDOWEJ
ŁAZIENKOWSKA
MYŚLIWIECKA
WAŁ MIEDZESZYŃSKI
AL SZUCHA
SZWOLEŻERÓW
Łazienki Park
CZERNIAKOWSKA
BARTYCKA
BANANOWA
NADWIŚLAŃSKA
SPACEROWA
PODCHORĄŻYCH
BLUSZCZAŃSKA
WOJSKOWEJ SŁUŻBY KOBIET
NEHRU
BELWEDERSKA
GAGARINA
IWICKA
CZERSKA
POLSKA
TRASA SIEKIERKOWSKA
CHEŁMSKA
PUŁAWSKA
DOLNA
BOBROWIECKA
WOLICKA
ANTONIEWSKA
JANA III SOBIESKIEGO
WITOSA
PLASECZYŃSKA
KALORYCZNA
BEETHOVENA
WINCENTEGO
POWSIŃSKA
BERNARDYŃSKA
TYNIECKA
Wilanów Palace
Wilanów Park & Gardens
Poster Museum

Wilanów Palace

Known locally as the Polish Versailles, the extraordinary 17th-century palace at Wilanów, although perhaps not quite living up to its French namesake, offers visitors to Warsaw both a glimpse behind how the Polish aristocracy once lived as well as a peaceful diversion from the frenzied roar of the capital. Just 10 km (6 miles) south of the city centre, the palace began life as a pet project of nobleman Stanisław Leszczyński, was quickly abandoned during the Swedish Deluge and was eventually bought by King Jan III Sobieski, who finished it in what is now considered to be the height of Polish baroque elegance. One of the country's greatest treasures, Wilanów Palace was ransacked by the Germans during World War II and lay in ruins until a mammoth restoration project (that continues to this day) saw it open its doors to the public in 1962. Now a museum that attracts scores of visitors daily, the building is stuffed full of Etruscan vases, bizarre coffin portraits, original frescoes,

The serene Wilanów Palace

antiques worth more than the annual GDP of many countries and much more besides. Slip on a pair of protective booties, grab an English-language audio guide and drift through the rooms, minding the schoolchildren as you go. Its popularity does have a tendency to turn the place into a rugby scrum at times, but the trip is worth it all the same. Give yourself at least 90 minutes for the palace, and expect the journey there and back on the bus to take up the same amount of time again. A highly rewarding visit awaits.

ⓐ ul. Stanisława Kostki-Potockiego 10/16 ⓣ 022 842 81 01 ⓦ www.wilanow-palac.art.pl ⓛ 09.00–16.00 Mon & Tues, Thur–Sat, 09.00–18.00 Wed, 09.00–19.00 Sun Bus: 116. Admission charge

WILANÓW PARK & GARDENS

Just as enjoyable for many who visit Wilanów Palace is a look around its superb 45-ha (111-acre) park and gardens. Highlights include delightful, two-tier baroque garden, which plays host to a series of outdoor classical concerts during the summer, the neo-Renaissance Rose Garden and the English Park, modelled on the classic English estates of the 18th and 19th centuries. The palace grounds also include the city's quirky Poster Museum (see page 96), the lovely 18th-century St Anne's Church, a boating lake and much more besides, all of which is mentioned on the palace's excellent website. With a little imagination, a basket full of food and a blanket, it's quite easy to spin a trip to Wilanów out into a full day's adventure.

CULTURE

Orthodox Church of St Mary Magdalene

This dazzling onion-domed church was completed in 1869 to serve as a place of worship for the Russian population brought in to work on the construction of the nearby train station. The church was one of only two Orthodox churches to survive an inter-war campaign to rid the city of its Russian heritage and its glittering golden interiors are guaranteed to draw gasps from visitors.

a al. Solidarnośći 52 t 022 619 84 67 11.00–15.00

Poster Museum (Wilanów Palace)

Warsaw's idiosyncratic Poster Museum is more than worth visiting if you're in the area. It features two halls connected by a courtyard, and walls plastered with the very best examples of

Detail from Wilanów Palace

the art form from all over the world.
ⓐ ul. Stanisława Kostki-Potockiego 10/16 ⓣ 022 842 26 06
ⓛ 10.00–15.30 Tues–Sun, 12.00–15.30 Mon ⓡ Bus: 116.
Admission charge

Railway Museum

Trainspotter Heaven, featuring a magnificent collection of model trains from Heath Robinson-style steam contraptions to the latest bullet trains. As well as the two rooms of displays including working train sets and a nice collection of model trams and cable-cars, find a massive assortment of rusting beasts in the garden out the back. Highly recommended, especially for children.
ⓐ ul. Towarowa 1 ⓣ 022 620 04 80 ⓛ 09.00–15.00 Tues–Sun, closed Mon. Admission charge

SD Galeria

Another Wilanów treasure, this charming little gallery inside a small cottage features a wide range of contemporary Polish art. Works vary from the ultra-serious to the downright comical. A pleasant diversion as well as a place to pick up a gift – if you've got money to burn.
ⓐ ul. Stanisława Kostki-Potockiego 24 ⓣ 022 842 00 66
ⓛ 12.00–20.00 Mon–Sat, closed Sun ⓡ Bus: 116

Warsaw Uprising Museum

Opened to coincide with the 60th anniversary of the Warsaw Uprising, this superb museum documents the city's rebellion against Nazi rule – a doomed two-month battle that saw the

population of Warsaw hasten liberation by rising against their Nazi overlords. The ill-fated rising cost the lives of more than 150,000 civilians, and left Warsaw little more than a heap of rubble. Packed with interactive displays, film reels and even a full-size replica of a B-24 Liberator plane, this museum will leave visitors in no doubt about the heroic tragedy Warsaw endured during the war. If you have time to visit only one museum, make sure it's this one.
ⓐ ul. Przyokopowa 28 ⓣ 022 539 79 33 ◷ 08.00–18.00 Mon, Wed & Fri, 08.00–20.00 Thur, 10.00–18.00 Sat & Sun, closed Tues. Admission charge

RETAIL THERAPY

Arkadia Central Europe's biggest mall and a lifeline for those starved of life's little luxuries. Aside from a range of designer stores occupying the top floor, the mall contains one of the few Marks & Spencer's food departments in the country, a 15-screen cinema and a good range of titles inside The American Bookshop. Anyone needing further inducements to visit should note that Poland's best microbrewery, Bierhalle (see page 102), is attached to the building. ⓐ al. Jana Pawła II 82 ⓣ 022 331 34 00 ⓦ www.arkadia.com.pl ◷ 10.00–22.00 Mon–Sat, 10.00–21.00 Sun

Bazar Na Kole A mecca for treasure-hunters, this outdoor market is just the place for anyone wishing to add a pre-war gramophone or a spiked Prussian helmet to their lounge. Antique curiosities galore with everything on offer from 1 zł vinyl records to palace doors from colonial India. Expect the unexpected and use your finest bargaining skills: pay the asking price and you can expect to be the butt of the traders' jokes come the end of the day. ⓐ ul. Obozowa 99 ◷ 06.00–14.00 Sat & Sun

Russian Market One of Warsaw's quirkiest attractions, though, unless you have an interest in counterfeit clothing and polyester trousers, it's unlikely you'll leave with shopping bags filled to bursting. Occupying the site of the former national stadium, the area became the focus of thousands of Russian and Vietnamese traders the moment the Iron Curtain was lifted, and the market is nowadays considered to be the largest outdoor bazaar in Europe. Unfortunately the market has fallen victim to numerous police clean-up operations, meaning that many of the shifty bootleggers selling dodgy items like pirate DVDs now find themselves staring at four walls, only to be replaced by traders selling useless accessories that will leave a trail of sparks flying if plugged in. Nonetheless an intriguing day trip, and one that may not exist for too long if the government get their way and close the market down. ⓐ Stadion Dziesięciolecia ◷ 06.00–14.00 Mon–Sat, closed Sun

TAKING A BREAK

Łysy Pingwin £ ❶ While comparisons to New York's Greenwich Village appear a trifle exaggerated, Warsaw's Ząbkowska street is enjoying an artistic renaissance, and this is where you'll find the local intellectuals wearing berets and taking their drinks.

Opened by a Swedish Buddhist, the Bald Penguin, as it is known in English, is every bit the eccentric venue one would imagine, with statues of Buddha, thrift store furnishings and screenings of underground films. The menu includes a series of homemade cakes while in summer the adjoining courtyard fills with local thinkers playing boules. As evening settles, unsigned DJs cut their teeth on the record decks. ⓐ ul. Ząbkowska 11 ⓣ 022 618 02 56 ⓛ 16.00–24.00 Mon–Fri, 16.00–03.00 Sat & Sun

Regeneracja £ ❷ Take a glimpse at Warsaw's alternative side in this interesting bar, café, club. Decorated with jumble-sale furniture and the work of disturbed local artists, this two-level venture features a limited budget-priced menu and walls and lampshades covered with pink fur trimmings. Visit at weekends to enjoy a completely bonkers music policy. ⓐ ul. Puławska 61 ⓛ 11.00–02.00 Sun–Thur, 11.00–04.00 Fri & Sat

W Oprachu Absurdu £ ❸ This place is a complete curiosity and proof of Praga's emergence as the home of Warsaw counter-culture. Popular with in-between-job actors and emerging artists, this foggy haunt can be identified by the black spider that hangs on the outside wall. Inside discover live bands and DJs hoping for their big break, while disinterested punters knock back spirits as they slump on theatre seats and assorted junk. ⓐ ul. Ząbkowska 6 ⓣ 060 691 42 65 ⓦ www.oparyabsurdu.pl ⓛ 12.00–02.00 Mon–Sat

Le Cedre ££ ❹ For a taste of the exotic head to Warsaw's right bank to enjoy premier league Lebanese cooking inside a warm interior that comes alive each Friday with the appearance of a gyrating belly dancer. Hookah pipes and jangly tunes add to the authenticity while the imported chefs do the rest of the legwork with cracking renditions of hot and cold Lebanese favourites. ⓐ al. Solidarnośći 61 ⓣ 022 670 11 66 ⓦ www.lecedre.pl ⓛ 11.00–23.00 Mon–Sat, closed Sun

Dom Polski £££ ❺ Loved by foreigners and locals alike, a detached pre-war villa plays home to this slightly formal restaurant. On long summer nights the garden is a must, while in colder climes sit inside amid posh manor-house decorations as impeccable waiters glide silently around delivering local delicacies like pheasant served with bison grass sauce. ⓐ ul. Francuska 11 ⓣ 022 616 24 32 ⓦ www.restauracjadompolski.pl ⓛ 12.00–23.00 Mon–Sat, closed Sun

Villa Rossini £££ ❻ The most ambitious culinary project Poland has ever seen can be found lurking behind the walls of this superb pre-war villa. Head chef and proprietor Frank Funke has created a masterpiece with this restaurant, with a series of rooms and chambers equipped with their own theme and menu – from Old Hanseatic dishes to modern takes on Polish cuisine. Individual touches include a private balcony for romantic trysts, mannequins standing in bathtubs and a garage converted into a beer bar. Prices can be considered steep by local standards, though they pale in comparison to the quality. Truly memorable. ⓐ ul. Tyniecka 16a ⓣ 022 844 21 90 ⓛ 12.00–23.00 Mon–Sat, 12.00–21.00 Sun

AFTER DARK

Bars & clubs

Lolek This circular bar could be easily mistaken for a Munich beer hall, what with all the clinking of glasses that goes on. ⓐ ul. Rokitnicka 20 ⓣ 022 825 62 02 ⓦ www.lolekpub.pl ◔ 11.00–03.00 daily

M25 This disused factory is evidence that Warsaw is fast catching up neighbouring capitals in the hedonism stakes. Fetish clothing is openly encouraged and the parties are legendary. ⓐ ul. Mińska 25 ⓣ 060 863 45 67 ⓦ www.m25.waw.pl ◔ Open only for one-off events

Skład Butelek In an area filled with people getting to the bottom of what Sartre really meant, the Bottle Bank, as it is known in English, makes for a refreshing break. This club affects the atmosphere of an impromptu squat party with edgy sounds. An essential visit. ⓐ ul. 11 Listopada 22 ⓦ www.skladbutelek.pl ◔ 19.00–03.00 Thur–Sat, closed Mon–Wed & Sun

Bierhalle A huge microbrewery responsible for Warsaw's tastiest and, hence, most dangerous beer. ⓐ al. Jana Pawła II 82 (Arkadia Shopping Mall) ⓣ 022 323 68 55 ⓦ www.bierhalle.pl ◔ 11.00–23.00 Mon–Thur, 11.00–24.00 Fri, 10.00–24.00 Sat, 10.00–23.00 Sun

Ornate clock tower in Poznań

OUT OF TOWN trips

Poznań

Traditionally regarded as the white-collar capital of Poland, Poznań is perhaps best known for its enormous trade fairs, which attract thousands of corporate bods each year from around the globe. But in spite of the surface seriousness and number of suits climbing in and out of blacked-out taxis this is by no means Hong Kong. Although Poznań's financial importance is easily apparent, its pristine old town has the sleepy atmosphere of a Bavarian backwater; the village ambience is light years away from the frantic flutter of the capital. By day a delightful place to potter around in, Poznań's historic centre stirs into life the

Poznań Opera House

moment the lecture halls and conference rooms empty as academics and business boys alike head into town to squander scholarship grants or enjoy expense accounts.

GETTING THERE

As Poland's trade fair capital, Poznań is easily accessible from the capital. Trains zip between the two cities regularly, with journey time taking under three hours. Poznań's train station, Poznań Główny, is directly west of the old town and depending on your material sensibilities is either a 10-minute walk from the centre or a 15 zł taxi ride. If you're travelling on, trains to Berlin run seven times a day. If time is of the essence, consider flying from Warsaw, a journey that takes less than an hour. See www.lot.pl for flight info. The airport is planted in the western nether reaches of Poznań with taxis to the centre ranging from 25 zł upwards – as with everywhere in Poland, avoid being ripped off by using licensed firms with big signs and logos splashed over the vehicles.

SIGHTS & ATTRACTIONS

Citadel Park

Directly north of the old town lies the Citadel Park, home of a network of 19th-century Prussian military fortresses. One of them has since been converted into the Poznań Army Museum and has an outdoor collection of military hardware. The southern reaches of the park contain a Soviet and Commonwealth War Cemetery, where among those buried are

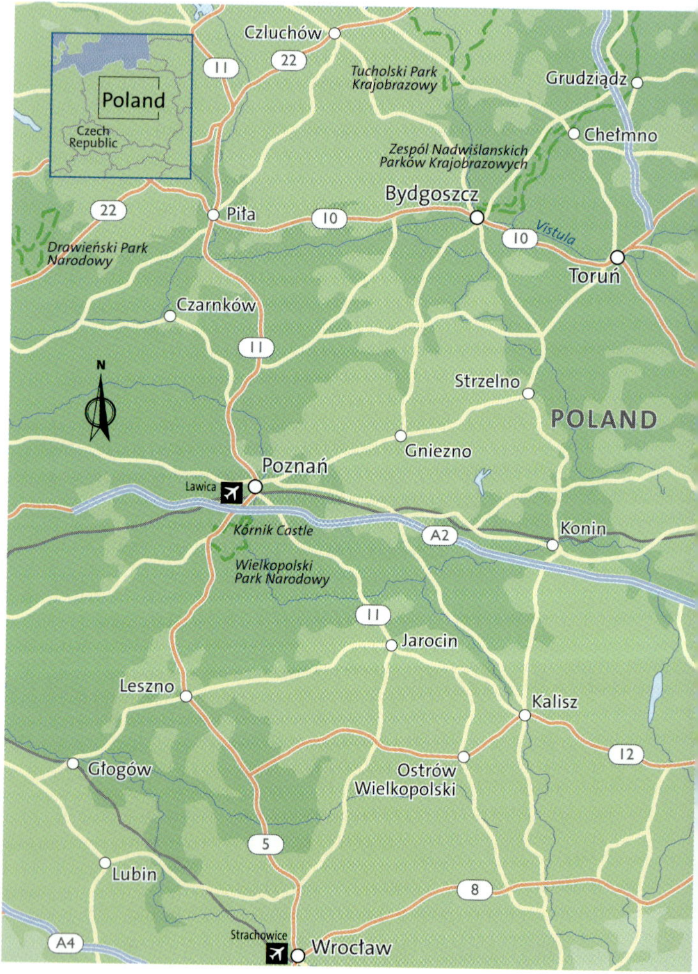
Poland
Czech Republic
Czluchów
22
11
Tucholski Park Krajobrazowy
Grudziądz
Chełmno
Zespól Nadwiślanskich Parków Krajobrazowych
Bydgoszcz
Piła
10
Vistula
Toruń
Drawieński Park Narodowy
Czarnków
N
Strzelno
POLAND
Gniezno
Poznań
Lawica
Kórnik Castle
A2
Konin
Wielkopolski Park Narodowy
Jarocin
Leszno
Kalisz
12
Głogów
Ostrów Wielkopolski
5
Lubin
8
A4
Strachowice
Wrocław

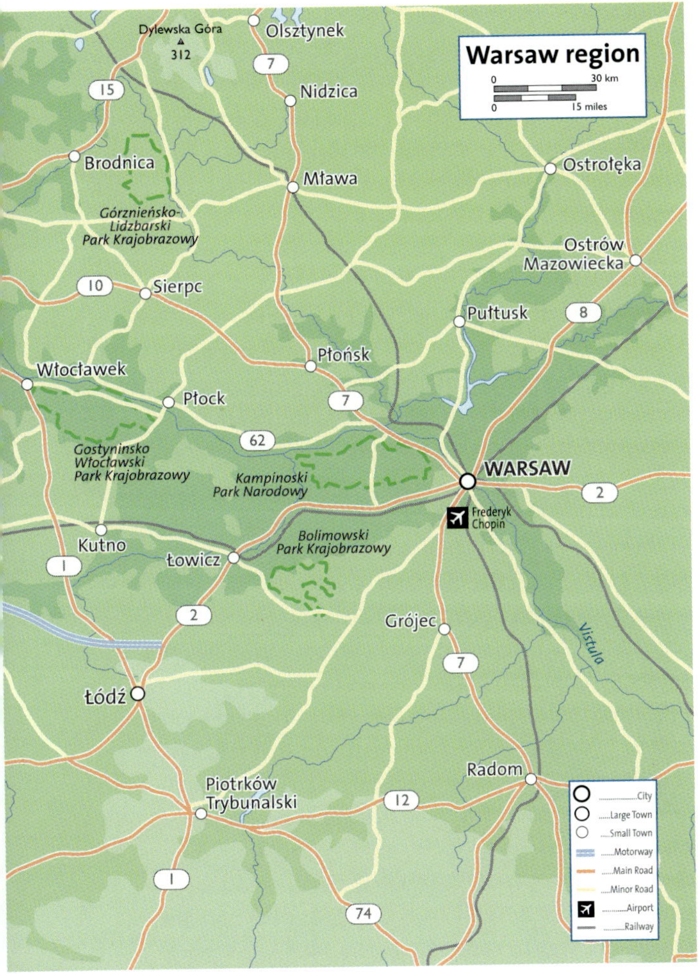
Warsaw region
0 30 km
0 15 miles
Dylewska Góra
312
Olsztynek
7
Nidzica
15
Brodnica
Mława
Ostrołęka
Górznieńsko-Lidzbarski Park Krajobrazowy
Ostrów Mazowiecka
10
Sierpc
Pułtusk
8
Płońsk
Włocławek
Płock
7
62
Gostyninsko Włocławski Park Krajobrazowy
Kampinoski Park Narodowy
WARSAW
2
Frederyk Chopin
Bolimowski Park Krajobrazowy
Kutno
Łowicz
1
2
Grójec
Vistula
7
Łódź
Radom
Piotrków Trybunalski
12
1
74
City
Large Town
Small Town
Motorway
Main Road
Minor Road
Airport
Railway

Allied airmen shot down over Poland during World War II, as well as many of those killed during 'The Great Escape' – which actually took place in the not-too-distant town of Żagan. One wacky artistic diversion comes in the form of 112 2-m (7-ft) tall headless figures that stand in the park; erected in 2002, the artistic interpretation of the controversial installation is open to debate.

Kórnik Castle

Rated as one of the great castles of Poland, the neo-Gothic Kórnik can be found 20 km (12 miles) southeast of Poznań with buses running every hour from the city centre. The journey costs around 5 zł with tickets available from the driver. Dating from medieval times, the castle owes much of its present appearance to the Działynski family who remodelled it extensively over the course of the 18th and 19th centuries. Although castle enthusiasts will find plenty to entertain them, it's advisable to hire a guide to get the most out of your trip; having strapped on a pair of oversized slippers you'll be taken through a series of impressive chambers that come packed with stories and legends – from a fireplace that was used by Tytus Działynski to hide from the Russian authorities, to a portrait of a white lady, said to come alive in the evenings. Curiosities range from Napoleon's spoon to a collection of medieval weaponry and a hunting room packed with oddities such as a Melanesian mask made using human bone.

ⓐ ul. Zamkowa 5 ⓣ 061 817 00 81 ⓛ 09.00–16.00 Tues–Fri, 10.00–16.00 Sat & Sun, closed Mon Ⓑ Bus: NB from the Św Marcin bus stop by Rondo Kaponiera. Admission charge

Statue of Jan Baptysta di Quadro, Poznań

Old Town Square

The old town square will act as your central gravitational point. Although it was largely destroyed during World War II, most of the townhouses were carefully restored during the 1950s maintaining their original Renaissance and baroque styles. The centrepiece is the old town hall – a giant Renaissance structure designed by Giovanni Quadro of Lugano and once hailed as the most beautiful building north of the Alps. Each day at noon you'll find crowds gathered outside to catch a glimpse of two tin goats that appear above the clock when midday strikes; the tradition dates from 1551 when two goats on their way to a cooking pot escaped and ended up stranded on the ledge of the town hall. Today the main building houses the **Historical Museum of Poznań** (ⓐ Stary Rynek 1 ⓣ 061 852 56 13 ⓛ 09.00–16.00 Tues, Thur & Fri, 11.00–18.00 Wed, 10.00–16.00 Sat, 10.00–15.00 Sun, closed Mon. Admission charge). This superb museum takes you through the history of the city – from its beginnings in the 10th century to the rebuilding efforts following the Soviet siege during World War II. Around the square the colourful jumble of townhouses is home to numerous restaurants and bars, as well as a motley collection of museums, including those dedicated to musical instruments, the Polish author Henry Sienkiewicz and the Wielokopolska Uprising of 1918 – a local insurrection against the ruling Germans.

Ostrów Tumski

Poznań is a city of churches, with the finest being clustered on the Ostrów Tumski island. According to historical sources this is where Poland's first bishopric was established in AD 968, and the cathedral crypt dates back to the founding of Poland, with famous corpses including that of Mieszko I, Poland's first ruler.

Further information

Explore Poznań online by consulting either ⓦ www.city.poznan.pl or ⓦ www.inyourpocket.com. The ubiquitous In Your Pocket also publish a tri-annual guide to the city with detailed listings providing an insider's-eye view of the city.

Tourist Information Centre

Your number-one source for maps, guidebooks and information, as well as the Poznań City Card, which, for 30 zł (one-day card), gives you access to public transport as well as the majority of local museums. ⓐ Stary Rynek 59/60 ⓣ 061 852 61 56 ⓛ 09.00–17.00 Mon–Fri, 10.00–14.00 Sat (only open one Sat per month), closed Sun

RETAIL THERAPY

The antique shops that line the streets of the old town make for an interesting diversion with everything from Roman coins to dusty 19th-century tomes on sale. If you want to keep pace with the local glamour pusses then a visit to the designer boutiques on ul. Paderewskiego is essential, while for a generic western shopping experience, consider visiting Stary Browar (ⓦ www.starybrowar.pl) – a large shopping mall housed in a former brewery dating from 1844.

TAKING A BREAK

Brovaria ££ On one side, a posh restaurant bursting with white linen and modern interpretations of Polish cooking; on the other side, a superb microbrewery set inside a modern space with views of the main square. Unmissable. ⓐ Stary Rynek 73/74 ⓣ 061 858 68 68 ⓦ www.brovaria.pl ⓛ 10.00–02.00 daily

Corcovado ££ The interiors are all brick walls and wooden clutter while the seasonal garden is the best in the business – complete with local artwork hanging from the trees. A café atmosphere prevails with coffee machines hissing in the background, though the upscale European menu deserves a mention of its own. ⓐ ul. Wroniecka 16 ⓣ 061 663 63 34 ⓦ www.corcovado.pl ⓛ 13.00–23.00 daily

Dom Vikingów ££ An impressive complex featuring a restaurant, bar, sports pub and café. It's a sleek environment with a well-presented modern international menu and a guaranteed collection of foreigners doing their best to impress local waifs with their stammering knowledge of the local lingo. ⓐ Stary Rynek 62 ⓣ 061 852 71 53 ⓦ www.domvikingow.pl ⓛ 09.00–02.00 daily

AFTER DARK

Kisielice A basement gem attracting a crowd who look like they've just finished band practice. This is the unofficial HQ of alternative Poznań with a pop art décor, experimental music sounds and regular screenings of complicated foreign films. ⓐ ul. Taczaka 20 ⓣ 061 665 84 84 ⓛ 10.00–01.00 Mon–Thur, 10.00–03.00 Fri, 18.00–03.00 Sat, 18.00–01.00 Sun

A Poznań square at night

Pod Minogą A legendary, and smoky, venue that fills with budding playwrights waiting for their big break. The interiors are theatrically decadent and the music policy is the most eccentric you'll find in town. ⓐ ul. Nowowieskiego 8 ⓣ 061 852 79 22 ⓛ 13.00–05.00 Mon–Sat, closed Sun

Proletaryat A commie-themed bar with a bust of Lenin sitting in the window and portraits of Mao and Uncle Joe pinned to the walls. A popular student haunt with some very good local beers on tap to help in your discovery of socialist paradise. ⓐ ul. Wrocławska 9 ⓣ 0508 17 36 08 ⓛ 13.00–02.00 Mon–Sat, 15.00–02.00 Sun

ACCOMMODATION

Mini-Hotelik £ Only 11 rooms to pick from, with access gained via a scummy-looking staircase zealously guarded by the hawkeyed caretakers. Budget-priced rooms are kept spotlessly clean and come with the smart look associated with European pensions. ⓐ al. Niepdoległości 8a (enter from the courtyard on ul. Taylora) ⓣ 061 633 14 16

Brovaria ££ A smart, upmarket hotel where beige-coloured rooms tout modern gimmicks and views of the old town square. The ground floor houses one of the best restaurants in town, as well as a microbrewery popular with expats and local big shots. ⓐ Stary Rynek 73 ⓣ 061 858 68 68 ⓦ www.brovaria.pl

Hotel System ££ A hi-tech mid-range effort with the faceless exterior of a modern office block. No need for laptops here, each room comes equipped with its own PC. One of the best deals you'll find, despite an off-centre location, and as such it is often fully booked with conference types. ⓐ ul. Lechicka 101 ⓣ 061 821 07 00 ⓦ www.hotelsystem.pl

Domina Residence **£££** Luxury apartments stocked with the latest techno gadgetry and a style plucked straight from the pages of a design mag. Living space and fully fitted kitchens in each, with a location on the border of the old town. ⓐ ul. Św. Marcin 2 ⓣ 061 859 05 90 ⓦ www.dominahotels.pl

Sheraton Poznań **£££** Opened at the end of 2006, the Sheraton's location next to the trade fair complex sees an endless procession of high-fliers trooping in and out – but once the business travellers have left, keep an eye out for cut-price weekend deals that allow the rank and file to enjoy 5-star luxury at slashed prices. ⓐ ul. Zwierzyniecka 3 ⓣ 061 655 20 00 ⓦ www.sheraton.pl

Łódź

The fabulously gritty city of Łódź, Poland's second biggest, was, until recently, the centre of the country's huge textile industry. Built from the sweat of the working classes and the brains of three men, the scores of smoky 19th-century chimneys are but all gone, having slowly been replaced with a new type of industry typified by swanky bars and art galleries inside Łódź's abandoned red-brick factories. With a disturbing Jewish past and a promisingly surreal future, American director David Lynch's favourite city offers a beguiling distraction and an utterly different destination altogether. Meaning 'boat', Łódź is pronounced *woodge*, a strange fact made doubly so by the fact the city has no river. Enjoy.

GETTING THERE

Pretty much in the centre of Poland, Łódź is criss-crossed with transport routes of all descriptions. Just 130 km (81 miles) southwest of Warsaw, getting here by train or bus is easy, although at the time of writing the rail route is undergoing some serious renovations, making the journey time ridiculously slow. Łódź boasts more than one main train station, so make sure you alight at Łódź Fabryczna, which is a few minutes east of the city centre. The bus station is next door. If you wish to make a flying visit, you'll be pleased to know that the national carrier LOT (w www.lot.pl) flies several times a day from the capital.

The Reformed Church, Łódź

SIGHTS & ATTRACTIONS

Księży Młyn Residence (Edward Herbst Mansion)

This isn't just a palace. It's a rambling conglomeration of industry and opulence and even a brief account of the history of the place could fill this entire guidebook. Briefly, however, what was once a humble mill on the river in the 14th century has grown, been handed down through generations, stolen, burnt down (twice), been the biggest mill in the region, powered by water, powered by steam, closed, reopened, turned into what amounts to a city and finally become the region's key tourist attraction. Central to it all is the residence of Edward Herbst (1844–1921), the one-time manager who thought it would be idyllic to doze off to the sounds of his machines whirring away weaving more wealth. Or maybe his wife, Matylda Scheibler, the daughter of the textile and energy magnate who had previously built the place up, thought it would be a good way to drown out his snoring. In any case, the estate now includes a mansion, various plants, both industrial and botanical, and workers' accommodation. There's also another palace-like bit that is somewhat more introverted and secluded and, probably, a better place to slumber. There's plenty to see here, so don't bother coming if you're in a great hurry. Or sleepy.
ⓐ ul. Przędzalniana 72 ⓣ 042 674 96 98 ⓛ 12.30–16.30 Mon, Wed & Fri, 10.00–16.30 Tues, 12.00–18.30 Thur, 11.00–15.30 Sat & Sun. Admission charge

Piotrkowska

This is the main drag, where everyone goes to see and be seen, exchange money for goods they didn't know they wanted and probably don't need, work, play and exchange yet more money for liquids that will make them bump into something on the way home. It carves Łódź in two, north to south, and can provide you with a captivating 5-km (3-mile) jaunt, making it one of the longest pedestrian streets in Europe. Not only is it studded with shops, restaurants, bars, cafés and tatty tin sheds selling things claiming to be kebabs, it's also home to an alluring array of crazy and quirky sculptures that will tickle the fancy of even the most devoted philistine. Rickshaws will happily zip you from anywhere to anywhere else along this strip for no more than 4 zł, the price of an end-to-end journey at the time of writing.

St Joseph's Church

It may be small, and dwarfed by the monstrous Manufaktura centre across the street, but, made from larch, it's kind of cute and even has a sweet little story to tell. The church was actually placed in its present location, bit by bit, by local factory workers during a night of generous industry and flurry in 1888. It was originally built in 1765–8 on Kościelny Square. There are conflicting suggestions about the construction of the free-standing bell tower. Some say it was built in the 18th century, which would give the whole church the honour of being the only pre-19th-century building in Łódź. Others reckon it was constructed from concrete in 1922 and then dressed up in a veneer of wood and charm. Who is right? God only knows.

ⓐ ul. Ogrodowa 22

JEWISH ŁÓDŹ

Łódź is home to what may well be the biggest Jewish cemetery in Europe, with some 180,000 people having come to rest here, and being more or less all that remains of what was once a huge and thriving religious and secular community. The cemetery even boasts the largest Jewish mausoleum (to the city's great industrialist Israel Poznański) in the world, as well as a hundred or so listed monuments. To get to the cemetery, take tram 1 or 6 north out of the city to the end of the line. The entrance is on Zmienna, west of the tram stop. The Synagogue was built in 1895–1900 and survived World War II by pretending to be a salt store. Another grim reminder can be seen in the Helenowek Orphanage, which is now a rundown dump but was a place of refuge for child survivors of the Holocaust. The old ghetto is located on Nowomiejska, just past Północna. Most of the buildings that formed the ghetto have been replaced by newer housing. The tourist information centre publishes an excellent free Jewish map of the city.

Synagogue ⓐ ul. Rewolucji 1905r. 28, ⓣ 042 633 51 56; Helenowek Orphanage ⓐ Krajowa 15

CULTURE

Textile Museum

The textile industry is intrinsically knitted into the history of Łódź, so popping along to the textile museum is a must if you want to

come away with any real knowledge of the city's history. Even if old steam-driven looms don't tickle your fancy (and how do you know if you've never seen one?) the museum is worth a visit simply for the location itself. The 5,000 sq m (53,821 sq ft) of exhibition space are sprawled out in a great big behemoth of a building dating back to the 19th century (it was whacked up in just four years, 1835–9) and still looking all pretty and white. It's a fine example of classicist industrial architecture.
ⓐ ul. Piotrkowska 282 ⓣ 042 684 61 42 ⓛ 09.00–17.00 Mon–Wed & Fri, 09.00–19.00 Thur, 11.00–16.00 Sat & Sun. Admission charge

Further information

Excellent online information can be found at both ⓦ www.cityoflodz.pl and the superb ⓦ www.inyourpocket.com. The latter also publishes a free guidebook to the city, *Łódź In Your Pocket*, covering everything from hotels to sights to clubs to shopping, and obtainable in many hotels throughout the centre.

Tourist Information Centre

A fabulous source of information including free brochures, books about the history of the city and really friendly and helpful staff.
ⓐ ul. Piotrkowska 87 ⓣ 042 638 59 55 ⓦ www.uml.lodz.pl
ⓛ 08.30–16.30 Mon–Fri, 10.00–15.00 Sat, closed Sun

RETAIL THERAPY

Despite the recent trend that is swamping it in restaurants and cafés, ul. Piotrkowska remains the main magnet for shoppers.

Surreal wall mural in Łódź

The newish Manufaktura complex (w www.manufaktura.com) is bursting with glitzy retail names and other treats, and despite starting life as a white elephant is destined to become something of a celebrity in town. In short, people don't come to Łódź to shop, but, as Poland goes, it does enough retail stimulation to keep all but the most demanding occupied.

TAKING A BREAK

Boston Café £ Smart, modern furniture, baffling modern art, good food and a stylish 20-something clientele make this not just a pleasant place to take a break, but one that offers a feast for the eyes as well. a ul. Piotrkowska 108 t 042 632 37 74 ⓒ 07.30–23.00 Mon–Fri, 09.00–23.00 Sat, 10.00–21.00 Sun

Coffee Heaven £ The best coffee in town, plus a pleasing flurry of snacks and light meals that will appease any palate. a ul. Piłsudskiego 15/23 (Galeria Łódzka) t 042 634 66 64 ⓒ 09.30–21.00 Mon–Sat, 10.00–20.00 Sun

Rooster ££ Skimpy blondes weave among booths studded with Americana, keeping everyone happy with a good choice of steaks and burgers that won't fit into even the most cavernous mouth. a ul. Piotrkowska 90 t 042 639 76 01 ⓒ 11.00–24.00 Mon–Wed, 11.00–01.00 Thur–Sat, 11.00–23.00 Sun

AFTER DARK

Łódź Kaliska Possibly the best nightspot in town, so it's a shame that you'll probably have such a good night here that you won't remember any of it. It's almost worth staying sober to ensure you actually notice and appreciate the awesome and varied array of live music, revellers and novelty wall-hangings. The mix of atmosphere, potent drinks and both weird and beautiful people makes this a must. Not to be missed, or remembered. ⓐ ul. Piotrkowska 102 ⓣ 042 630 69 55 ⓛ 12.00–02.00 Sun–Thur, 12.00–04.00 Fri & Sat

Peron 6 If it's beer you want, you won't find a better place anywhere in Poland. The refrigerators are glistening, crammed and clinking with the best of beer brought in from far and wide, so you can indulge in a global pub crawl without leaving your seat. Fortunately, the stairs at the door lead down on the way in and up on the way out, which is all for the best when you consider the tricks that gravity and alcohol like to play at the end of a good night. ⓐ ul. Piotrkowska 6 ⓣ 042 639 80 19 ⓛ 12.00–02.00 Sun–Wed, 12.00–04.00 Thur–Sat

ACCOMMODATION

Linat Orchim £ Run by the local Jewish community, the Linat Orchim is your best choice for budget accommodation, with a series of well-kept private rooms, as well as larger rooms featuring added frills. ⓐ ul. Pomorska 18 ⓣ 042 632 46 61 ⓦ www.linatorchim.zgw.lodz.pl

Geyer 'White factory', factory, Łódź

Orbis Grand ££ A grand location in the middle of the city, esteemed former guests include Roman Polański and Heinrich Himmler. An old-fashioned but elegant air, and not to be missed if you can get a room. ⓐ ul. Piotrkowska 72 ⓣ 042 633 99 20 ⓦ www.orbis.pl

Trams are a great way to explore the city

PRACTICAL information

Directory

GETTING THERE

By air

Previous centuries saw Warsaw dubbed the 'crossroads of Europe' and it's a moniker that still applies. Warsaw Okęcie Airport is serviced by all major airlines, with BA and LOT flying from London Heathrow. LOT's budget offshoot, Centralwings, flies to London Gatwick. The next-door terminal, Warsaw Etiuda, handles budget flights and carriers include Wizz, Sky Europe, easyJet and Ryanair, with destinations including Manchester, Birmingham, London Luton, London Stansted, Glasgow and Dublin. For a full flight schedule refer to Ⓦ www.lotnisko-chopina.pl

Many people are aware that air travel emits CO_2, which contributes to climate change. You may be interested in the possibility of lessening the environmental impact of your flight through the charity Climate Care, which offsets your CO_2 by funding environmental projects around the world. Visit Ⓦ www.climatecare.org

By train

The central train station (Warszawa Centralna) is one of Europe's least salubrious, though it has numerous international connections, with the most high-profile being Berlin, Bratislava, Budapest, Moscow, Prague and Vienna. If travelling on overnight trains, bear in mind the reputation they have earned for robberies and theft – invest in a sleeping berth to avoid nasty surprises.

By road

By European standards, the Polish road network is sub-standard. There is no intercity motorway system, so roads are single-carriageway and generally extremely congested. Warsaw itself has no bypass, so all traffic is routed through the city centre. For more information about driving in Poland, contact the **Polish Motoring Association** (022 629 83 36). It also provides emergency roadside assistance, as well as breakdown and repair services.

ENTRY FORMALITIES

All European Union passport holders and citizens of Australia, Canada, the United States and New Zealand can enter Poland and stay for three months (six months for UK and other EU citizens) without a visa. Since joining the EU, Poland's customs laws have, if anything, become more confusing than they were before accession. Those leaving Poland and heading for another country within the EU can allegedly take a maximum of 10 litres (2.6 gal) of spirits, 90 litres (24 gal) of wine, 110 litres (29 gal) of beer and 200 cigarettes with them, but you might find the customs official in the country you arrive in disagreeing with the maths. People planning to fill their luggage with what might possibly be considered contraband are advised to contact the appropriate embassy before doing so.

MONEY

At the time of writing, Poland is still using the złoty, and Poland's finance minister has gone on record declaring that a switch to the euro is not likely before 2010. For UK travellers the złoty has consistently hovered at around 5.5 to the pound, and you'll find €1 will usually buy 4 złoty. Bear in mind that Poland's rocky track record in economics means that these figures are liable to fluctuate. ATMs are widespread and all will offer an English-language option, and Visa and MasterCard are widely accepted. If you want to exchange currency then be on the lookout for *kantors* (exchange offices). Rates vary widely, so shop around. Breaking big notes can present problems in smaller shops, so it's advisable to carry small change.

HEALTH, SAFETY & CRIME

Although there are no obvious dangers associated with visiting Warsaw, visitors should be on guard against nimble-fingered pickpockets who've turned their black craft into an art form. Don't leave your phone exposed on a table, and never leave your

Polish currency: 1 złoty = 100 grosz

wallet or documents in an unattended jacket. Traditionally Warsaw's right bank, Praga, has been regarded as cowboy country, and ostentatious shows of wealth will attract the attention of the meatheads you may see lurking in the courtyards. Use common sense. The tramps and vagrants you see rummaging through bins and urinating in their trousers are part of the furniture and generally harmless. Black-clad cops with luminous yellow jackets keep a high profile in the city centre and should not be messed with. Although you'll find few that speak English, they do a decent job of keeping the locals in line (though do have an irritating habit of picking on tourists for jaywalking).

Considering the wages and working conditions, Polish doctors do a grand job of keeping the hospitals up and running, though a bribe is still standard for anyone wishing to jump queues. The many private clinics and hospitals offer a fully westernised standard of service with rates to match. A visit to a GP in a private clinic will start at 100 zł for a consultation. For lesser ailments there are a few 24-hour pharmacies scattered around, including one on the top floor of the central train station.

The tap water is safe to brush your teeth with, though it's best to opt for the bottled variety if you're looking for a drink.

OPENING HOURS

On the whole most shops operate from around 10.00–18.00, while office hours are usually set at 09.00–17.00. Banks stay open slightly longer, though you'll be lucky to find one open on a Saturday. Museum opening hours require a degree of guesswork, with impossible-to-remember opening hours regularly changed to suit the season and the whim of the curators. As a rule, most close on Monday. The majority of restaurants, bars and clubs stay open until the last guest leaves, and many will have no hesitation in bolting the doors if business has been slow. By the same rule, as long as there are people lingering you can expect many venues to keep serving way beyond sensible hours. If you want to experience the glories of one of Warsaw's many markets then set your alarm clock, as most are strictly morning affairs.

TOILETS

Visitors will generally find toilets marked with a circle for ladies and a triangle for men. Public facilities are rare, though you will find bathrooms in the train station and airport. These tend to be guarded by stern old women who will expect a fee in return for admission, regardless of the odious surprises that sometimes lie in store.

CHILDREN

Although most Poles welcome children, travelling with kids in Poland can be a chore, with many restaurants and shops lacking in high-chairs and nappy-changing facilities. You'll find nappies and other baby essentials widely available in supermarkets. Most of the 5-star hotels hold extravagant brunches each Sunday afternoon, with expat families turning up en-masse to enjoy the feeding frenzy. Adults get to enjoy mountains of food and limitless booze, while the younger charges have a dedicated kids' corner complete with a qualified multilingual babysitter, games, films and special menu. Although the cost for adults is usually in the 120 zł range, the cost for the munchkins is usually either set at half-price, or sometimes even free. The **Marriott**

(@ al. Jerozolimskie 65/79) and the **Sheraton** (@ ul. Prusa 2) are commonly regarded as the best in the trade.

Arsenał An Italian restaurant in close proximity to the old town is the stage for Warsaw's most family-friendly eatery. In winter children are limited to a playroom by the entrance, though in summer the options increase with an outdoor playground complete with monkeybars and slides. @ ul. Długa 52 (enter from ul. Andersa) ⓣ 022 635 83 77 ⓦ www.restauracjarsenal.pl

DH Smyk Poland's most famous kid-specific department store. Clothes, books and toys pack the corridors, and there's a separate 'mother and baby' room as well. @ ul. Krucza 50 ⓣ 022 551 43 00 ⓦ www.smyk.com

Poles love children and child-friendly facilities are becoming more common

Wodny Park Rated as Warsaw's best pool. Waterfalls, a 72-m (236-ft) water-tube and a separate children's area with an elephant-shaped slide keep the kids in high spirits, and even the suburban location should not deter a visit.

COMMUNICATIONS

Telephones

Payphones are now so relatively expensive compared to other forms of calling, and are generally broken when you finally manage to locate one, that using them to keep in touch is no longer a realistic option. Much more advisable are the multitude of Voip services offered by all but the lowliest of Warsaw's internet cafés (see page 136) and/or buying a local SIM card. All three Polish mobile operators offer prepaid mobile services, each of them cheap to get up and running and not too costly for sending text messages and making the occasional call inside Poland. Assuming you have an unblocked mobile phone you can currently buy a SIM starter pack from all companies for 8 zł. Top-ups start at just 5 zł. Find them for sale at mobile company shops (see below), in many kiosks and at the airport, train and bus stations.

Era ⓐ ul. Puławska 15 ⓣ 022 413 44 44 ⓛ 10.00–19.00 Mon–Fri, 10.00–14.00 Sat, closed Sun

Orange ⓐ pl. Konstytucji 6 ⓣ 022 628 84 52 ⓛ 09.00–20.00 Mon–Fri, 10.00–17.00 Sat, 10.00–16.00 Sun

Plus GSM ⓐ al. Jerozolimskie 148 ⓣ 022 882 02 02 ⓛ 10.00–21.00 Mon–Sat, 10.00–20.00 Sun

TELEPHONING POLAND

To call Warsaw from abroad, dial your international access code (usually 00), then the national code for Poland (48), followed by the area code for Warsaw minus the initial 0 (22) and the local number. Somewhat confusingly, the prefix 022 at the start of a telephone number is both the code for Warsaw and a part of the number. So, if you're calling from one Warsaw landline to another you'll need to include the 022 at the beginning. Likewise, if you're calling Warsaw from another city in Poland, dial the 10-figure number starting with 022. If you're calling a landline from a Polish mobile, just dial the 10-figure number. If you're using the Plus GSM service, drop the first 0.

TELEPHONING ABROAD

To phone home from Warsaw, dial the outgoing code (00), followed by the relevant country code (see below), area code (minus the initial 0 if there is one) and local number.

Australia 43
New Zealand 64
Republic of Ireland 353
South Africa 27
UK 44
USA & Canada 1

National enquiries t 912
International operator t 901

Internet

Casablanca Offers all manner of internet services as well as karaoke evenings. ⓐ ul. Krakowskie Przedmieście 4/6 ⓣ 022 828 14 47 ⓛ 09.00–01.00 Mon–Fri, 10.00–02.00 Sat, 10.00–24.00 Sun

Cyber Café Prices are steep but the lobby café next door sells the best espresso in town. Handy if you need to check email as soon as you arrive. ⓐ ul. Żwirki i Wigury 1 (inside the Courtyard by Marriott hotel) ⓣ 022 650 01 72 ⓛ 24 hours

Simple Zillions of flat screens and a chip-card payment scheme. One of the best – if not *the* best – in Warsaw at the time of writing. ⓐ ul. Marszałkowska 99/101 ⓣ 022 628 31 90 ⓛ 24 hours

Post

Poland's postal service can be painfully slow, so expect mail heading for the UK to take up to a week or more to arrive. Postboxes are red and have a yellow post horn on a blue background. At the time of writing, postcards and letters cost 1.30 zł to send inside Poland and 2.40 zł to all other destinations worldwide.

Central Post Office (Urząd Pocztowy Warszawa 1) ⓐ ul. Świętokrzyska 31/33 ⓣ 022 505 33 16 ⓛ 24 hours

ELECTRICITY

Electricity is reliable and all of it is 220 V, 50 Hz, AC. To get your plug in a socket you'll need a round, two-pin European adaptor. People travelling from the United States might also need a transformer.

TRAVELLERS WITH DISABILITIES

Travellers with disabilities might find visiting Warsaw tricky; facilities for disabled people are only just starting to appear, thanks to EU legislation. Warsaw's main hotels are all more or less fully equipped with wheelchair access, though many bars and restaurants – even the premium-priced ones – are yet to bring themselves into line.

For further information try the following organisations:

Disabled Persons Transport Advisory Committee
Ⓦ www.dptac.gov.uk/door-to-door

SATH (Society for Accessible Travel & Hospitality) US Ⓐ 347 Fifth Ave, Suite 610, New York, NY 10016 Ⓣ 212 447 7284 Ⓕ 212 725 8253 Ⓦ www.sath.org

Trip Scope UK Ⓣ 0845 758 641 Ⓦ www.tripscope.org.uk

FURTHER INFORMATION

Tourist information centres are few and far between with the exception of the old town. As well as the two listed below, you'll find another inside the main international arrivals hall at the airport (same opening hours as below). The city's official tourist information website is Ⓦ www.warsawtour.pl.

Tourist Information Centre (old town) Ⓐ ul. Krakowskie Przedmieście 39 Ⓣ 022 94 31 Ⓛ 08.00–20.00 May–Sept; 08.00–18.00 Oct–Apr

Tourist Information Centre (train station) Ⓐ al. Jerozolimskie 54 Ⓣ 022 022 94 31 Ⓛ 08.00–20.00 May–Sept; 08.00–18.00 Oct–Apr

Emergencies

MEDICAL SERVICES

Chemists

The following chemists should be open 24 hours. Call in advance to confirm.

Apteka 21 ⓐ Central Railway Station, al. Jerozolimskie 54 ⓣ 022 825 69 86

Apteka 2000 ⓐ ul. Widok 19 ⓣ 022 827 35 93

Apteka na Banacha ⓐ ul. Banacha 1a ⓣ 022 823 64 11, ext. 1033

BEATA ⓐ ul. Solidarności 149 ⓣ 022 620 08 18

EMERGENCY NUMBERS

Ambulance ⓣ 999

Fire ⓣ 998

Police ⓣ 997

It's unlikely anyone at the other end of the three numbers listed above will speak English. However, the good news is that the Polish police now operate a daytime and evening emergency call centre for foreigners in English and German that closes around the time you'll probably need it. Call from a local landline on ⓣ 0800 20 03 00, or if roaming ⓣ +48 22 601 55 55 ◷ 08.00–24.00. Your best bet for a knight in shining armour will come in the form of your embassy. Brits should call the switchboard on ⓣ 022 311 00 00 while Americans will need ⓣ 022 625 14 01

Dentists

Dental Centre ⓐ ul. Ludna 10 ⓣ 022 625 01 02

Dental Centre ⓐ ul. Radiowa 1a ⓣ 022 638 97 48

Dentalux ⓐ ul. Racławickat 131 ⓣ 022 823 72 22

CONSULATES

Australia ⓐ ul. Nowogrodzka 11 ⓣ 022 521 34 44

Canada ⓐ ul. Matejki 1/5 ⓣ 022 584 31 00

New Zealand ⓐ al. Ujazdowskie 51 ⓣ 022 521 05 00

Republic of Ireland ⓐ ul. Humańska 10 ⓣ 022 849 66 33

South Africa ⓐ ul. Koszykowa 54 ⓣ 022 625 62 28

United Kingdom ⓐ al. Róż 1 ⓣ 022 311 00 00

EMERGENCY PHRASES

Help!	Pomocy!	*Po-mo-ste!*
Fire!	Pożar!	*Po-jar!*
Stop!	Stop!	*Stop!*
Call an ambulance/ a doctor/ the police/ the fire service!	Wezwać pogotowie/ lekarza/ policję/ straż pożarna!	*Ve-zvach po-go-toh-vyeh/ le-ka-jah/ po-lee-tsyeh straj po-jar-nom!*

The publishers would like to thank the following individuals and organisations for providing their copyright photographs for this book: Ejdzej & Iric/SXC.hu page 130; EmoEmo – FOTOLIA page 117; HuBa/Wikimedia Commons page 125; Hubert Śmietanka/Wikimedia Commons page 34; Jaroslaw Adamczyk – FOTOLIA pages 103, 104, 109; Pictures Colour Library page 19; Richard Schofield pages 3, 9, 42–43, 96; Robert Tomczak – FOTOLIA page 113; Visit Poland pages 29, 36, 90; Wikimedia Commons page 122; World Pictures page 7; all the rest Don Egginton.

Copy editor: Jenni Rainford
Proofreader: Ian Faulkner

Send your thoughts to
books@thomascook.com

- **Found a great bar, club, shop or must-see sight that we don't feature?**
- **Like to tip us off about any information that needs updating?**
- **Want to tell us what you love about this handy little guidebook and more importantly how we can make it even handier?**

Then here's your chance to tell all! Send us ideas, discoveries and recommendations today and then look out for your valuable input in the next edition of this title. As an extra 'thank you' from Thomas Cook Publishing, you'll be automatically entered into our exciting prize draw.

Send an email to the above address (stating the book's title) or write to: CitySpots Project Editor, Thomas Cook Publishing, PO Box 227, The Thomas Cook Business Park, Coningsby Road, Peterborough PE3 8SB, UK.